MW00491216

ISBN13: 978-1-932045-33-8
ISBN10: 1-932045-33-3
LCCN 2022909046
First Edition Paperback 2022

Strider Nolan Media, Inc.
6 Wyndham Way
Lancaster, PA 17601
www.stridernolanmedia.com

SHADOW S.E.A.L.

John Watts

with Michael S. Katz

Strider Nolan
MEDIA

The author's extended family

DEDICATIONS

To my God and Father Jesus Christ,
For teaching me and showing me, I am a work in progress.

For My Wife,
She is my shield and my armor. When I was unable to read, she taught me by reading the Bible. When my PTSD would raise its ugly head she would bring calm back into my life. She is my point person always guiding me to Jesus and his path.

To My Mother,
Who gave birth to me and set me on a moral path.

- John Watts

PROLOGUE

They called me Shadow because they weren't allowed to call me Nigger.

In the '60s, the military had an unwritten policy against using racial epithets to demean recruits. However, officers tended to follow the policy more than non-commissioned officers. My SEAL drill instructor had no reservations against using the N word. There were times that the word Nigger effortlessly rolled off his tongue. But this emboldened the other recruits to do the same, and I believe he put a stop to their harassment not for my sake but for the sake of the Team. So rather than call me Nigger he called me Shadow.

I was the only black man in my SEAL class. I can still see the hatred for me on the white faces. In fact, most of the white faces I looked at during my military career—from boot camp to SEAL training to my service during the Vietnam War—pretty much had that expression on their faces, where the N word was just shooting out of their eyes and boring into my brain like a drill. I could almost hear their thoughts saying, "He has no place being here."

And there wasn't a single thing I could do about it. No standing up for myself like in the movies. No great comeuppance for the bigots and bullies. No, I had to just take it, because things would only have gotten worse for me if I had stuck up for myself.

Funny thing is, it wasn't until I signed up to serve in the Navy, to put my life on the line for my country, that I learned for the first time just what white people thought of me. Growing up I hadn't been exposed to a lot of racism. And when I was, it didn't even really register with me.

CHAPTER 1
MY EARLY LIFE

Birth of a Frogman.

February 1, 1948. I was conceived in the embryonic fluid of my mother's womb. When the time came and the fluid was released, I was set free with a war cry that hailed the birth of a new frogman. Born for war and ready to fight.

I grew up in North Philadelphia, one of the roughest parts of the city. Philadelphia was a downer due to the struggle any family had to face just to get by, to make ends meet, and to stay in the city.

In these testing times, my life swirled me in different directions. Some days, city life would just leave me bewildered and wanting more out of it. Other days, the city would let me spread my wings and help me grow in ways I couldn't even imagine. Looking back, I realize my life has changed drastically from what I was to what I am.

In the City

Slave ships transported Black people from Africa to Philadelphia and Virginia. My great-great grandparents were victims of slavery, and many subsequent generations were subjected to unjust treatment in the city.

In the heart of North Philadelphia, a mostly black and Latino neighborhood, stands Girard College. The school was named after multi-millionaire Stephen Girard, whose fortune came from shipbuilding, banking, and the slave trade. Upon Stephen Girard's death in 1831, per his will, he left seven and a half million dollars to the city of Philadelphia to ensure completion of a college. Finished in 1848 and sitting on 43 acres, the private school was surrounded by an eight foot high stone wall and was open to poor white orphan boys. No girls or minorities. The institution was a breeding ground for racial profiling and prejudice and was not integrated until 1966, after protests from the Black and Latino neighborhood.

Protesting had actually started earlier. In 1964, increasing tensions in North Philadelphia soon escalated into restless protests. There were hardly any jobs for the Black community. Police brutality grew more prevalent. There was no access to the basics of life, no industries in the neighborhood. Everything was so hostile toward minorities that it made life static.

When they weren't just pushing to survive, Black people lived with dignity and desired a positive change, a better experience. Our neighborhood was home to many Black families who took pride in their houses and streets. They would always strive to do everything in their power to keep life safe and the city clean.

There were no white people living in North Philadelphia when I was growing up in the 1950s, at least none that I knew of. The only white faces were teachers and those people who owned businesses. The neighborhood had no stores owned by Blacks.

There was one white man named Mitchell who owned a men's clothing store, where my dad would work part time during the holidays. That is where I learned how to dress for success. I would get all my suits and dress shirts from the store. Mitchell was a good guy to everyone. During the race riots in the mid-60s, his was one of the few stores left standing.

I was never called the N word in Philadelphia, but whenever I would go down to South Carolina to visit my great-grandfather's farm, I would be subjected to derogatory remarks based on my race. That's where I got my first taste of racism.

Before I was allowed to go south to see my great-grandparents, I was schooled on how to behave, what to say and what not to say, who I could look at and who not to look at. I had to learn to pretend that white people were better than me just so I could be safe.

We were made to get off pavements and walk on the street if a white woman started walking down the same path. There were signs so people could know what places Blacks could eat or drink in the town. Being young I did not know what a big deal it was until the time we were refused service in a store and made to drink from water fountains that dogs drank out of.

A lot of this was new to me. Our family did not face any racial prejudice while we grew up in North Philadelphia. We did not even know we were considered poor because our father and mother supplied everything we needed.

Family Pride

The Watts family all shared the same initials, J.W. My father, John Watts, married my mother, who happened to have a similar first name, Johnnie Ruth. I was the oldest of five children, named John Watts Jr. Then came Jeffery Allen Watts, Jerome Ross Watts, Jacqueline Ruth Watts, and Joyce Michelle Watts. It wasn't until August of 2004, while my father was in hospice, that I learned I'd had another brother: a half brother named Alan Chesnutt.

My father owned a bootblack shop just around the corner from our house. He worked with two helpers to polish and shine shoes. On Saturdays my brother Jeff and I would often visit our father's shop to get our shoes polished for church.

My father owned the business for quite a while before landing a regular job for Philadelphia Electric Company. He was first responsible for cleaning the coal yard, coal being the source for electricity. My Uncle George then helped my father get a "hopper" job: he was responsible for putting coal dust in the hopper where the coal was used to generate electricity.

Dad was later promoted to yardmaster. He oversaw operations in the coal yard and the electricity-generating area. At the time, he was able to earn a fair amount for a Black man, making over $10,000 a year, before he was forced into retirement when he was diagnosed with lung cancer.

From the vaguest corners of my memory, I remember how the roof of our house once caught fire. Scorching flames filled the sky, but my mother risked her life to go back into the house and get my father's paycheck from the bedroom. I remember the fire department had tried to stop her from entering the house, but to her every paycheck could mean the difference between having a home and living in the street.

My mother was a risk taker; she let go of a lot to keep us all safe and preferably at home. She held our family firmly together and maintained a strong bond among us. All her life, she protected the people she loved the most. Everything we are is because of her; she saved us all from breaking apart in tough times.

I can picture my mother staring toward the horizon, very visibly holding hope in her eyes from afar. She was the main person in my life who let me see I could achieve my dreams. Every now and then I found myself turning to her for inspiration and support. She became the strength I always needed in every phase of my life. For me, she has always been a beacon of hope in the most challenging stage of my life, my teenage years.

Family Ties

It is hard to narrate how close my family has always been. Perhaps we have all had an inseparable bond. We had an eternal loving connection that I cannot even hope to express in simple words. Our mom always talked about staying as one big happy family.

My siblings and I all had a ride-or-die mentality. We caused so much havoc and trouble for our parents with all our mischief! But we were equally protective of each other, too. Living together, we watched each other helping Mom and Dad, and sometimes unknowingly annoying them, which is why our bond always remained a beautiful truth.

There was no free living concept in the Watts Family. Everyone had to work every day. At a very early age, I learned how to stoke a fire in our coal furnace. After the burned coals cooled, one of my brothers and I would go down the basement to collect unburned coal pieces from the ash.

My brother, Jerome, was a natural born salesman. To earn a living he used to hustle fresh chicken and eggs, sometimes fish, off the back of a truck. His pay was based on the number of sales he made in a day.

Jerome used to work so hard to master new basketball skills. He was taller than Jeff and me. The money Jerome made let him buy a pair of Chuck Taylor sneakers. Back then, they were about eight dollars a pair, a lot of money to pay for sneakers! The best my other brother Jeff and I could afford was Red Ball Jets, but we still thought we were the fastest guys on the block.

Jeff was a huge troublemaker, but with good intentions. He was accommodating, and would always help Mom and Dad any way he could. But anytime he would try to help around the house, something would go south.

Our family did not own a frost-free refrigerator freezer. Ice would build up on the sides, making it hard for us to get food from inside. Jeff was always willing to help with defrosting the refrigerator freezer. I vividly remember how he started by pouring a bucket of hot water into the freezer to melt the built-up ice. It seemed like a relatively slow and tedious process to me, but like I said, we all had to pitch in with household chores. One day, Jeff accidentally chipped a hole in the freezer and ruptured the tubing. He panicked immediately because one of the freon tubes had badly ruptured. Jeff was scared, expecting he was going to get a spanking (which he ultimately did). We tried everything to plug that hole: bubblegum, glue, whatever we could get hold of. We even got Dad's soldering iron and tried to solder the gap closed, but nothing we tried could prevent the valuable gas from leaking out. In the end, Dad had to buy a new freezer and refrigerator. Although Jeff got his butt handed to him that day, I still look back at it and chuckle.

Jackie and Joyce were much younger and calmer than us boys. I remember them playing with their dolls or imitating our mom when playing with their girly house and cooking toys.

Saturday was house cleaning day. We had to scrub, mop, and wax the floor. We used Ajax cleanser to wash the white-marbled front steps of our house. Mom would come to inspect our work by swiping her fingers over the steps to check for cleanser residue. We had to wash and scrub the steps all over again if even some residue was left.

While carrying out household chores, we always sang:

Two hours pushing brooms and mops;
Gee, this woman doesn't know when to stop.
Man, o man, this woman is the queen of the house.

Mom would pretend to get so angry at us but she knew it was all in good fun and humor.

Allowances would be distributed after the house cleaning. Mom would hand out a fifty cent allowance to boys and twenty-five cents to the girls. We used to spend our allowances on the movies. We would all take off running down the street to the Pearl Theater, where it was fifteen cents to get in. We would sit there in the movie hall from noon to 5 because it was the house rule that you had to be home before dark. We would watch cartoons together, old serial stories like *Rocket Men*, Buster Crabbe's *Hercules* and westerns. We never got tired of watching any of those.

We knew we had to be home before dark, before the streetlights would illuminate the neighborhood's dark streets. One Saturday afternoon we decided to stay later than usual because we wanted to see what the adults were watching. I remember the story was *Imitation of Life*. I think it was about 6 or 7 p.m. when Mom came down to the movie theater searching for us. She wanted to see what we were doing there. She slammed through the theater gate, the usher following her clacking heels up and down the aisles until she found us. I'd had my arm around some girl, but I jumped up out of my seat like a jack-in-the-box when I heard her calling our names. My mom made me take off my belt at the theater and she whipped our asses all the way back home.

For Love of Water

It was the mid-1950s, and we were the only Black family on our street to own a color T.V. set. Watts children were excessively obsessed with T.V. shows as well as movies. Since we were the only house on the block with a color T.V. set, we hosted the Sunday *Mickey Mouse Club* cartoon matinee for kids in the neighborhood.

One of my favorite T.V. shows was *Sea Hunt* with Lloyd Bridges. Bridges played Mike Nelson, a former Navy frogman turned freelance underwater diver. He hunted for treasure, tracked down drug traffickers, and performed other heroic feats. I loved watching him put on his diving gear and going out to save those in need. I desperately wanted to learn how to scuba dive myself; the world underneath the seas just seemed fascinating to me. I was always captivated by the things the protagonist would do, and dreamed of being able to accomplish such feats in my own life.

I never paid much mind to the passage of time as I got older. Picnics, Christmas, birthdays, everything was always celebrated; each celebration was an excuse for a family reunion. On Father's Day we would arrange a family picnic, all uncles, aunts, and cousins getting together. Every year, our family meet-up point would always be the same giant oak tree at Philadelphia's Fairmount Park. We would have breakfast, lunch and dinner outside at the park. We would play badminton, volleyball, dodgeball, baseball, horseshoes, and anything else we could think of. Some of the adults would play cards.

I, for one, loved being in the community swimming pool, Kelly Pool. It always had my undivided attention; the feeling of water freed my mind and soul. It was all I looked forward to every year, as it was only once a year I got to enjoy the thing I loved doing the most: being in the water. I spent most of the picnic hours in the pool, imagining myself as Lloyd Bridges diving with tanks and fins. I'm sure Mike Nelson set many a viewer on the path to wanting to explore the undersea world.

My father and I would race the width of the pool and every year he would beat me by a full length. This made me push harder, looking forward to the day I would beat my dad.

My father's brother, Sam Watts, and a man named Adolphus Louis got together and bought a camp in the Catskill Mountains in New York. The camp was called Camp Mohawk. The kids that went there were from well to do Black families; doctors, lawyers, judges. The cost of the camp was $500 for the summer, which was a lot of money in the early '60s.

I worked there in the summer washing dishes and I was allowed to participate in camp activities when I wasn't working. The camp had a very large pool and I practiced swimming every day, along with karate. My skills in both improved quite a bit. Kids at the camp knew I worked in the kitchen, so they would try to put me down because I did not come from money and did not have the air of sophistication that they flaunted. I may have been from the 'hood and washed dishes, but I could outswim and outfight them all. Plus, the girls at camp found me attractive and pursued me, which I enjoyed.

When my dad came for a visit, we had another swim meet. This time I beat him by more than a length. The very first time! My father told me I cheated, that I jumped the gun, and he wanted a do over. We raced again and I beat him a second time. He finally relented and said, "Son, you beat me fair and square."

John and Johnnie Ruth Watts

CHAPTER 2
SCHOOL DAYS

My siblings and I went to the same schools. We did our elementary schooling at Douglas and were together in Simon Gratz High School.

My brothers and sisters had minor problems with schooling, but I was not a good student at all. I barely got by in English and mathematics, but I at least liked science, social studies, history and geography. However, I unknowingly suffered from dyslexia and my learning problems were never diagnosed back then. So I faced significant problems identifying speech sounds and learning how they related to letters and words. I could hardly read anything!

Later on, I realized that I might not be an excellent reader but I was an outstanding visual learner. I learned to push my way through by any means. And if it wasn't for Mom tutoring me or hiring tutors for me, it could have been a lot worse.

Outside of school, my friends and I had one favorite sport, baseball. Every kid on the block owned a baseball glove. We would go to 25th Street and the Diamond recreation center to play.

In the fall we played football. I still have a scar on my lip from playing all those years ago. One time during a game I grabbed Jeff by the leg for a shoestring tackle. He pulled out of my arms and stepped on my bottom lip, puncturing a hole through it. Unfortunately, Mom and Dad were at work that day. I had to seek medical assistance myself. At the time I was dating a girl, Elaine Francis, who happened to be a year older than me. I went to her house, and her mother took me to the hospital to get my lip stitched. The scar never went away.

Kids Will Be Kids

After I healed, all of the guys got together for a celebration party. Someone came up with the idea of forming a neighborhood boys only club. Jackie, my younger sister, insisted on getting into the club. She was always stubborn. It was mean of us, but us boys mocked her for wanting to join.

We thought we could give her something challenging to do, something to embarrass her, so she would not want to join our club. We told her she could get in our club if she walked around the block wearing football shoulder pads and a boy's jock strap. Much to our surprise, she did exactly what she was told to do. She was not easily embarrassed. We had no choice but to let her into our (no longer boy's) club.

My mother became in charge of it, now called the Mill Boys and Girls Club. We would go out and collect newspapers, clean people's yards and basements, and give all the hard earned money to her. Then once a year, Mom would take us to the park for a big picnic with hamburgers, hot dogs, and ice cream. Other times she would take us on trips to the zoo and the museums. She always found something for us to do. She was not only my mom but a surrogate mother to all the kids on the block.

There was a mean old lady who lived on the block. We called her Nosy Berkeley. We were throwing around a football in the street in front of her house and the ball rolled onto her pavement and hit her steps. She came out of the house, grabbed our ball, and went back inside. Back in those days, footballs were made of real pigskin. She soaked the ball in water until the pigskin surface of the ball was ruined, then came back out and returned it to us.

We met around the corner in a vacant lot and plotted our revenge. One boy dropped a paper bag full of dog shit on the steps of her house, another set the paper bag on fire, and a third rang her doorbell. Then we all hightailed it to safety, hiding behind a car to watch. When Ms. Berkeley came out to answer the door, she was wearing her furry slippers. She stomped the fire out like a crazy woman, and when she was done she had dog shit all up and down her slippers. We were all cracking up behind the car, laughing so very hard and trying not to be heard at the same time!

In junior high school, I was the lead in the school play, *The H.M.S. Pinafore*. I was captain of the swimming team. I also realized I was pretty good at mechanical drawing and always had a flair for art.

In high school, I sang in the school choir and ran cross-country track. I played football and represented the gymnastics team. I was unfortunately still not good at learning other things. With time and undivided attention, I became a talented artist and chose Arts for my major. I studied drawing and art techniques and entered poster contests for different banks and city organizations such as the Philadelphia Savings Fund Society, PSFS. I never won a poster contest but I did come in second one year.

Jeffery, Jacqueline, Jerome (with
daughters), Alan, and Joyce.

CHAPTER 3

MARTIAL ARTS

At the age of 11, I unexpectedly met two of my best friends, twins Thomas and Joseph Anglin. The twins were two years older than me, but still our friendship was very close. We hit it off quickly and became lifelong friends.

I once went to a neighborhood recreation center with Thomas and Joseph. There were two guys who taught martial arts there, Joe Grant and Benny Welborn. They were black belts in combat judo, a Japanese martial art. The twins had met the instructors in a local market and happened to have been their first students. They introduced me to the instructors and I joined the class. With focus, determination, and undivided attention, I soon became good at this sport as well.

At the age of 16, I earned my first black belt for Shotokan Karate, another Japanese martial art fighting style. Tom, Joe, Benny and I would go around the city, giving demonstrations. I remember we once performed at a cabaret club for adults. It was a BYOB, where you brought your own liquor — whisky, wine, vodka, anything you fancied — and enjoyed music and dancing. We got up on stage and did our rendition of the Chinese roots of karate.

We recreated a story of bandits constantly harassing monks traveling across China's mountains, stealing their food and goods. Among these monks was a Shaolin master who taught others the ancient art of fighting to defend themselves. During the reenactment, Joe had to pretend to reach down to grab my testicles and rip them off. As Joe pulled his head back, he kept on firmly grasping my pants and did not let go. He tore a massive hole in my pants. The only thing I had on was my jock strap, with everything else hanging out.

Dealing With Gangs

Philadelphia had a ton of gangs. Tom, Joe, and I would often take on menacing gangs in the neighborhood. The three of us would often face off against 8 to 10 boys at a time. It was always a great feeling knowing we could beat that many guys. In no time, we built our reputation in the neighborhood.

One of the scariest gangs in Philadelphia was the 24th Street Gang, famous for their cruelty and viciousness. They would cut you as soon as look at you. One day, the 24th Street Gang approached and asked us to join. You had to "jump in" to join their gang. This meant the new recruit must fight someone and knock them out. But the three of us were not interested in being in a gang. We wanted to stop the menace that the neighborhood gangs created in the area, especially the gang terrorizing 24th Street.

Tom, Joe, and I decided we would fight the entire gang. We took our positions, back to back to back. A roundhouse kick streaked at one of the gang member's faces, making his mouth bleed. A knife hand into the neck of another sent him down. One gang member connected with a punch to my jaw and I felt a little woozy, but I shook it off, quickly recovered, and threw a flawless double dragon knuckle punch to his chest. It knocked the breath out of him and he dropped to the ground. After a few minutes of fighting, the gang called it off and promised to never terrorize the block again. I had been privileged to have Tom and Joe standing by my side to help me save my block.

In high school, I continued learning and mastering martial arts. I was proud I had a black belt at 16. Before I got into martial arts, I remember being bullied by this kid at school, Israel. He would kick my ass, riding, walking, coming and going. Sometimes I ran away from him and his friends to keep from fighting them, but my mom was persistent. She took me down into the basement once and tried to teach me how to box. She even made me go out and face him every time he confronted me. When the time came that I excelled at martial arts, he confronted me and got his earned beating. I kicked his ass. He stopped messing with my siblings and me after I beat him a few times in a row.

CHAPTER 4
THE TROUBLE
WITH GIRLS

When I was 13 I had a girlfriend, Elaine Frances. She had a very light complexion, as did her parents, both of whom were from Jamaica. Her parents did not think much of me because I was too dark compared to them. Imagine that, racism from my fellow Blacks.

Elaine was very smart. She went to Girls High School, an institute for some of the best and brightest girls in Philadelphia. I took her to her prom as well as my own. I would sneak into her house at night while her parents were asleep, and we would make out and fool around.

We went together for years, actually, until I was in boot camp. One night while I was in training my mom found Elaine and a friend from boot camp kissing and making out on the sofa. Needless to say we broke it off. More on that later.

Graduation photo of the author

CHAPTER 5
MY CHILDHOOD DREAM

In 1965 the country was at war in Vietnam, and I was about to graduate high school. In school I was an art major and good at making maps. I had a chance to go to Drexel University to study photo-geography (that's making maps from photos). I visited the college and was told my eyes were not good enough but my scores made me a good candidate for engineering.

I went back to my school and talked to my guidance counselor, a white woman named Mrs. Hoiberg. She told me engineering was not a good fit for me. I would be learning how to fix cars, and it was not a good profession.

Meanwhile the military draft was going on. I was not interested in going into the Army or the Marines. I was interested in the Navy since I had always loved the water and I wanted to learn how to SCUBA dive. I knew that I wanted to be a diver in the Navy, it had been my passion for so long. It was my childhood dream from watching Lloyd Bridges in *Sea Hunt*, and from all those hours spent swimming.

Three weeks before my high school graduation, I went to the Navy recruiter and enlisted. I was 17 years old and required my father's permission to join the Navy. It took quite a lot of convincing to get my father to sign the enlistment papers. At the time, he probably assumed that I just had a temporary bee in my bonnet and would soon get over it in a few days.

To convince my dad of my intentions, I had to prove to him that I was capable enough to progress in my life. I had to graduate in order to prove my worth to him. Back then, in high school, I was having a tough time passing my math class. So when I realized that I was not going to pass math because I was going to flunk an upcoming exam, I went to my math teacher and begged her to give me the passing marks. I told her that if I failed the forthcoming exam, I was going to have to drop out of school, and that would be bad for my future prospects. Quite reluctantly, she accepted my plea and gave me the passing grade to keep me from dropping out of high school.

After that, things escalated quickly. Graduation was set for June 18th, and I was quite keenly looking forward to it because my departure for Naval boot camp was set for June 21st.

On the morning of June 18th, my mom woke me up to get dressed. She attended my graduation with me; my father couldn't participate in the ceremony due to his work commitments. After graduation I spent the next three days with my family, as I knew I would tremendously miss them during the three months that I had to spend in boot camp.

On the morning of June 21st, I woke up with a rush of thrill and excitement. I had to report to the recruiter's office by 8 a.m. I knew that if there was one thing that the military is exceptionally stern about, it is punctuality.

The Navy provided a list of things I was permitted to bring, and I had packed my stuff the night before. So when I woke up I was raring to go. I took a quick shower and prepared for my departure. The entire morning no one spoke a word at the breakfast table. The atmosphere was grim.

Just when I was ready to leave the house and had reached the door, my father stopped me and said, "Why do you even want to go into the Navy anyway? It is a waste of your time and life. Black men like us do not do anything but wash the officers' uniforms, cook their meals and clean up their cabins. They don't even have the slightest of respect for men of our color, our race!"

My father's words stung me badly, but I had already made up my mind about the Navy. I knew it was what I really wanted to do.

I arrived at the recruiting station by 7:50 a.m. with my mother, who had come to see me off. Lines of young men about my age, some even older, crowded the station's hallways. By 8:05 a.m., several buses arrived and took us to the Greyhound bus station, which was located at 17th and Market. Besides myself, there were a few other Black guys on the bus going to boot camp. These boys were from Germantown, a section of Philadelphia.

My mother waved at me as the buses departed for their destination. My father was nowhere to be seen.

Early Navy photo of the author.

CHAPTER 6
BOOT CAMP

Boot camp — the Naval Training Center — is located west of the Great Lakes in Michigan. We drove all day and into the night until the buses stopped at the Great Lakes boot camp. It had been a one-day trip to our destination, as we reached it the very next morning from when we had departed.

As soon as we got off the bus, a loud voice pierced my ears. There was a young Petty Officer who bellowed at us to form queues on a white line painted on the ground. He called us maggots and other salacious names, our harsh introduction to how everyone would be treated in training.

The first thing we did was go to an orientation seminar. Then we were distributed our uniforms by the Quartermaster: bell bottom pants, long sleeve denim shirts, and white Dixie cup hats. After that, we were divided into groups and assigned to Petty Officers. Our respective supervising Petty Officers took us to our barracks. All of our clothes and personal items were put into big bags and mailed back to our homes that very same day.

The following day when we woke up, they took us to the base's hospital to get shots for allergies and other conditions. One thing that stood out was the "flying seven": rather than needles, they used air guns to inject whatever it was they shot into our bodies, pinching the gun in our butts and arms. After that, they conducted physical examinations. The physical exams and injections took most of that day. We had four hours of training afterwards.

The next day was when we would learn about the chain of command. There were about 85 of us in the classroom, and only six of us were Black: myself, the four guys from Germantown, and Willie Hodge from Albuquerque, New Mexico.

Willie sat next to me in class. He was a fast talker and a bit of a con man. He could sell you the Brooklyn Bridge if you listened to him long enough.

Willie is the guy who my mom caught cheating with my girlfriend at my own house! Months after we met we had been stationed at the Philadelphia Naval shipyard. Willie came to my house one day but I wasn't there. I don't know for sure how he met Elaine, I just assume she stopped by to see me and my mom introduced Willie as a friend of mine from the Navy. Smooth talking Willie did his thing and my mom found him and Elaine making out on the sofa. And that's why I broke it off.

Us and Them

At the end of the chain of command class, our drill instructor directed us to elect several people from our platoon for special positions. One man would be the master at arms, another would be the platoon leader, and a third would be the guard of arms. Of course, all the candidates were white.

As I mentioned, only six of us were Black. There was immediately an us versus them mentality in our barracks. The hostility was heavy in the air. As a group of young Black guys, we had to find a way to exert ourselves.

Since I had never really been around white people growing up in North Philly, I did not quite know what to expect from them. But I knew that I had the skills to outfight, outrun, and out-muscle anyone. From the age of 16 when I earned my first black belt in Shotokan karate, I was highly confident about my skills and strength. No one there knew of my martial arts background until I put forth my push to be alpha dog in the barracks.

I remember standing on one of the tables in the barracks and challenging anyone who wished to take me on in a one-on-one fighting competition. Several people accepted my challenge since they assumed by my external demeanor that they would easily take me out. All of them failed as they fell to the ground and tapped out. Only one white boy from Texas even came close to taking me on. He had been a high school wrestling champion. This dude put me in a lock that stretched my chest out, restricting my breath. But I worked my way out of his lock very smartly and ended up defeating him.

Not everyone was impressed, and I was made to stand down by the Drill Instructor. Still, after winning the challenge, I took the position of the guard of arms. I would be responsible for carrying the platoon flag and sometimes also calling cadence.

At boot camp we did a lot more than just marching. Navy boot camp is not like Army or Marines training. There is a lot of classroom work, about 65 to 70 percent. Field work was the other 30 percent or so. In the beginning the classroom work was light stuff like the chain of command, shipboard behavior, fire drills, how the decks are numbered, that type of thing. We trained on how to march in formation. We also learned firefighting in case a fire ever broke out on a ship.

They taught us hand-to-hand combat and we trained vigorously. At the time karate was pretty much an unknown fighting skill. As the drill instructors taught us the use of judo style combat techniques, I in turn taught them karate. I had also previously been trained in judo but tended to rely more on my karate skills. I wound up excelling in both styles. The instructor was impressed and wanted to know how I had learned and who trained me. His exact words were, "How did a little Nigger like you learn fighting skills like that?" He did not like me showing him up in front of the other recruits.

During our training we also learned how to use the M16. We learned how to break it down, rigorously clean it, put it back together, and professionally fire it. We went for target practice at least three times a week. I had never fired a weapon before, so it took some time for me to get used to being good at it. However, I honed my shooting skills as time progressed.

Sometimes when we would screw up, the Drill Instructor would make us do extra push-ups, or order us to put our hands up under our armpits and run around the playground saying, "I am a little ship bird, tweet, tweet, tweet."

We also ran obstacle courses and practiced strength training. We spent time in the tear gas chamber learning how to deal with being exposed to tear gas if the situation ever arose. Moreover, we did a lot of work in the pool, learning how to swim and staying underwater for prolonged times.

My Big Chance

Then came the call for recruits who wanted to pursue diving as their main focus. No one in my class answered this call except for me. To prove my skills, I was taken to the pool and told to perform different styles of swimming. They made me do a variety of strokes to see how far I could swim and for how long I could tread water without a break. After this, they put a 20 pound pack on my back and told me to breaststroke across the pool. This was the most challenging task of all.

I thought I did well on the test, but the instructor told me he didn't think I had what it would take. He said that I couldn't swim fast enough and that my breaststroke was weak. After a little while, he added that my American crawl was also weak. I was brokenhearted. I knew my potential well enough, and I realized that the only reason he was disrespecting me was to make up excuses because of my skin color. According to his mentality, I shouldn't have even been able to attend boot camp at all, let alone be able to swim this well.

I knew I had been turned down because of my skin color. They never even gave me a chance to get better, if indeed I did have to improve in any areas. But I wasn't willing to give up. I deserved far better, and I was well aware of my worth. Even though I was exceptionally discouraged and disappointed after my instructor turned me down, I decided I would not give up, no matter what. Since boot camp was three months long, I had plenty of time to improve my swimming abilities.

I devised a plan to accomplish my goals. After that day, I spent all my free time in the pool and at the gym, perfecting my strokes and building my stamina. I was not going to let that instructor have the last word and kill my dreams simply because he despised me for my skin color.

I continued to challenge myself and the guys in my platoon by having informal competitions with them. I tried to stay focused and avoided getting a big head. Eventually my hard work paid off and I was so obviously good that the instructor had to pass me.

As the boot camp was ending, our drill instructors picked the top recruits. I was totally shocked and surprised when I was chosen as one of them. I left the boot camp with an E2 rank, one rank below Private.

After boot camp I had the privilege of attending the engineman school in Norfolk, Virginia. Naval enginemen maintain and repair ship engines. The school was eight weeks long. During that period of time I learned to fix and maintain turbo diesel engines, working on six hundred and seventy-one engines in all.

Around the World

After I completed the course at the engineman school, I was assigned to the *USS Oglethorpe*, an AKA-100 Andromeda-class attack cargo ship. After reporting to the *Oglethorpe*, the superiors thought it was better to assign me to an assault boat crew as an engineman. In April of 1966 we left for the Mediterranean. The crew of the ship was looking forward to visiting countries throughout Europe. The ship was also carrying 1,600 Marines from the 1st battalion.

During that time, we were going to prepare for battle in the Vietnam conflict along with the Italian and Greek navies. Our first stop was Rhoda, Spain. The ship refueled there before proceeding to our next stop, Barcelona. We docked in Barcelona for about two weeks, where we were granted the liberty of doing whatever we wanted.

Some of my crewmates and I heard about a festival happening nearby in Pamplona, Spain. It was called the Running of the Bulls, and at that time we had no idea what it was all about. We took a train to Pamplona, only a few hours ride from where we were residing. Once we got off the train, we found ourselves in the middle of several bulls wildly running down the main street. You could hear the animals coming as the roads vibrated due to their heavy hooves pounding a rhythm into the concrete. In the background you could hear music, people hooting and cheering, and women screaming.

The men were dressed in white with red sashes around their waists. We easily fit in with the crowd because we were in our summer whites and Dixie hats, color coordinated with the residents. The next thing I knew, we were running down the streets with everybody else. Believe me when I say that this was a big adventure for a young Black kid from North Philly.

In a few hours, our ship left for Cannes, France. Cannes is where they have the famous Cannes Film Festival. I had never been to a place like that before. The maximum traveling I had ever done as a kid was when I went to South Carolina to my great-grandfather's house and New York to visit my grandmother. But as we walked down the Main Street in Cannes, France, the feeling was very different. The beach was on our right, and stores were on the very left. As we looked out over the beach we saw it was packed with people who were sunbathing. Many of the women were topless, which kind of just blew my mind. At the time, I just did not know how to react to that. I had never seen any topless women in my entire life.

The next port of call was Naples, Italy, a beautiful and interesting city located not too far from Mount Vesuvius. We also went to the island of Crete, where we had a beach party. I tried beer for the first time during that party. The beer we had was Heineken's, and it was delicious.

During that time, I had an opportunity to meet up with my Uncle Donald, my mother's brother. He was in the Air Force and had been stationed on Crete.

After we left Crete we headed for Istanbul, Turkey. It was then, about two months into this Mediterranean cruise, that I received word that I had been accepted into the Navy SEAL boot camp. Orders were cut for me to fly out of Istanbul back to Coronado, California, home of the Navy's amphibious base, to report to the SEAL Team One quarterdeck.

CHAPTER 7
HISTORY LESSON

From the age of ten, in 1958, when I started watching *Sea Hunt,* I wanted to learn how to SCUBA dive. Anything that had something to do with diving I watched, and I worked hard to improve my swimming.

As I got older, I learned about the Navy's Underwater Demolition Team. I believed that joining the Navy and becoming a UDT man would satisfy my desire to become a diver. UDTs were the Navy's elite sailors. The UDT built their reputation as an elite unit in World War II and the Korean War. During World War II, UDTs cleared the beaches and the inland areas of German mines and the ocean floors of concrete obstacles that would prevent Allied landing craft from bringing troops ashore. In the Pacific, UDTs again distinguished themselves with their actions on the Pacific islands, clearing beaches of mines, performing reconnaissance in the jungles, and setting up radio stations.

Many of these men didn't even carry firearms because at the time the military did not have waterproof guns. These men would often be sent out on missions with nothing but shorts and knives.

In 1942 the Navy requested volunteers to form a new unit to learn landing craft and beach reconnaissance. That Navy unit was then combined with Army Raiders and called Navy Combat Demolition Units, Scouts and Raiders.

During the Korean War, UDT assignments went further inland, blowing up railroads and munitions well beyond the beaches, even searching for and rescuing prisoners of war in North Korea. These UDTs were called frogmen because they wore all-green scuba suits.

It is widely believed that President John F. Kennedy created the SEALs (for SEa Air Land), but that is not quite true. SEALs were an evolution that started back in 1942. The first SEALs were volunteers from various UDTs. Members of the Underwater Demolition Teams were already some of the best at commando-style fighting and small scale military tactics.

The military was looking for a group to engage in unconventional guerrilla warfare where necessary. President Kennedy, a Navy hero himself, knew of the importance of the evolution of warfare. Communism was expanding and wars were changing. No longer were battles to be fought in large waves of infantry and tanks. Guerrilla warfare was the future.

The military invested a large amount of money in new forms of warfare, especially special operations like the SEALs, the Army Green Berets, and Marines Force Reconnaissance Units, to fight during the Cold War.

Navy SEAL Teams One and Two were formed in January 1962. Team One was established at Coronado, California to handle operations in the Pacific Ocean. Team Two was established at Little Creek, Virginia, and tasked with Atlantic Ocean operations.

The first recruits came from UDTs. They trained in Sea, Air and Land tactics. Airborne and land operations were new additions to UDT training, which became called by the designation BUD/S: Basic Underwater Demolition/SEALs training.

SEALs represent the best of the best; the most confident; the most intelligent; the most focused. I read once that

SEALs tend to come from families with high expectations for them. That wasn't me. My father and uncle had thought I was crazy for wanting to be in the Navy to begin with, let alone trying to become a SEAL.

CHAPTER 8
IN THE FACE OF
PREJUDICE

I flew from Istanbul back to the states, a bundle of nerves. Being a SEAL was not a done deal; the final decision on my selection was going to take place in San Diego, California. I was anxious because I really wanted to be in the SEALs.

SEAL Training

The SEAL base was located in the San Diego Naval Warfare Center and I was going to be in Seal Team One's quarterdeck. After I arrived in San Diego, I checked in and was immediately shown the bunk where I would be spending the rest of my days in Basic Underwater Demolition/SEAL (BUD/S) training.

The following day we went to a giant room where we received our workout gear. After that, we were shown the concrete grinder, the area where we were supposed to exercise relentlessly every day. I also saw a replica of the monster from the movie *The Creature from the Black Lagoon*. If you do not know the beast, it was a man-shaped swamp creature with huge gills and a fish mouth that would terrorize people on shore. The movie was released on March 5, 1954. Someone with a weird sense of humor had erected a statue of the creature outside the main building. It was holding a sign shaped like a trident saying, "So … ya wanna be a frogman".

There was also a large brass bell. Any time that a trainee decided to give up on the BUD/S program, they were required to ring the bell. It was the ultimate act of shame.

Hello, Shadow

During my first day on the grinder, I saw that I was the only Black guy who had been chosen for the team. My Master Chief immediately started calling me Shadow, which deeply bothered me. Navy regulations would not allow him to call me a Nigger, so his way around that was giving me the nickname Shadow. I can still hear the Master Chief in my mind saying things like, "Looks like we got a shadow in here."

The other recruits then started calling me Shadow, yelling things like, "Hey, Shadow, can you cook? Hey Shadow, can you make beds and wash our clothes?"

This racism bothered me a lot, but at least it was better than being called Nigger. Worse was how I was sidelined and thought of as inferior to the rest of the team. They would never have mocked another white person that way.

Our Drill Instructor immediately put a halt to this type of chatter when he heard of it. I appreciated that, even though it shouldn't have started in the first place.

But again, I was so determined, I decided that I was not going to let a bunch of white guys push me around. Although I thought I deserved a chance to show them what I was made of, I let it go. I let it go because we were going to be on the same team for a while and I didn't want any more resentment towards me. I was going to show them what I could do through my actions. I would show that I could swim, that I could run, that I could shoot, and that I could fight better than anyone else. I was not afraid, and I was not going to let them make me afraid.

Every day we got up at five o'clock in the morning, and after breakfast we went on a three mile run. After that, we did sit-ups and push-ups. The beach behind the SEAL Team One quarterdeck had large dunes where we would run evolutions in the sand, up one dune and then down the other side.

Evolutions were hour-long exercises turned into assignments, sometimes with a specific purpose, sometimes just for the sake of working our muscles. For example, we were made to run with 150 pound logs on our shoulders. Boat crews were put together to run with 170 pound, 13 foot long rubber rafts sitting directly on our heads. You might run two evolutions with the raft on your head, each evolution to take one hour. Evolutions in the San Diego Harbor could be three and a half hours of free swimming and a half hour of fast boat pick up.

Boat crews were made up of six to eight men, all about the same height. Surprise, surprise, no one wanted a Shadow on their boat crew. During the runs, I would get yelled at, being told that I was not pulling my weight. They did not think I had the fortitude to complete training and would say things like, "Shadow, just ring the damn bell now and give up. It will save you time and save our lives later." I hated these comments but it motivated me to prove them wrong.

Training Surf Passage was extremely hard, as I had to learn how to manage a 170 pound boat in heavy surf. When the boat filled up with water, it could weigh as much as a small car. The crew spent more time being spat out into the ocean than we did sitting in the boat. We would do this all day and all night until we made one beach landing with a full crew.

In the ocean we would often lock our arms and kick our legs in a rhythm, making sure to keep our heads up and out of the water. We would run laps up and down the beach, struggling all the while. The sand made running hard, and our legs grew tired to the point we could not even walk, so we would stop from time to time and lay down in the surf with just our shorts, shirt and life jackets on. After that, they would make us roll over in the sand, which was known as "making sugar cookies." This training went on for several weeks.

After this was over, we started working on weapons training. We all learned how to use AR-15s, M16s, 50-cal machine guns, 45-cal sidearms, the Stoner 63 machine gun, M-14, M79 grenade launcher and the 12 gauge pump shotgun with beehive rounds. They would time us on how fast we could put the M16 back together.

If we were lucky, we would get to go to bed at 11 o'clock at night after being awake since 5 o'clock in the morning. It was really tiring at the start but we got used to it.

We would get three meals in a single day and would only have five to six minutes to eat each meal. You could see everyone just gulping down their food, eating as much as possible in the short time we had.

We had swimming every day, not in a pool but in the wide open Coronado Harbor. The harbor temperature would range from 55°F to 70°F. The water was very, very cold.

None of my crewmates talked to me. They did not want to be bothered by me at all. Since I was a person of color, all around the SEAL academy there were several rumors floating about me. I heard demeaning things like I did not have good night vision since I was Black, or I had excessive body fat. I even heard that Blacks were just simply not good at swimming. What my teammates did not know was that I was a part of the All-City swim team in Philadelphia. I swam for Vaux Junior High School and then the All-City High School. Our school won several championships because of me, and I was proud of that. I was not concerned about my swimming capabilities as I was well aware of what I could do. No matter what they said, I didn't doubt myself because of my past achievements.

CHAPTER 9
HISTORY LESSON

I knew I had what it took to be a Navy SEAL, no matter the color of my skin. I wasn't the first, either, although I didn't know anything about what it had been like for my predecessors.

William Goines

William Goines was the first Black man to join the Navy SEALs. He was inspired to join the Navy when he saw the 1950 movie *The Frogmen* but he had to finish high school first. He enlisted in 1955 and started frogman training with a group of 96. Goines was one of only thirteen men to complete the training.

When President Kennedy formed the SEALs in 1962, Goines was one of the forty men chosen to join Team Two. He served three tours in Vietnam. He would have served a fourth tour but his valuable Spanish speaking skills got him transferred to another duty.

Goines retired from the Navy in 1987, after 32 years of service. Over his career he was awarded a Bronze Star, the Navy Commendation Medal, the Meritorious Service Medal, a Combat Action Ribbon and the Presidential Unit Citation.

Fred Morrison

Engineman Second Class Fred Morrison came before Goines. Morrison was a member of the Navy's Underwater Demolition Teams, the first Black man to serve in the UDT. Out of 115 sailors who tried out for the UDT in 1945, the man nicknamed "Tiz" was one of only six who completed the course.

Morrison served in World War II and the Korean War, where he earned the Bronze Star for heroism. After the Korean War he became a UDT instructor, where he was given the nickname "Fearless Fred, King of the Frogmen." After nineteen years in the Navy Morrison retired in 1962, so he was not part of the SEALs by the time they were formed.

CHAPTER 10
FRIENDS AND FOES

Eventually I made two friends in BUD/S. First there was Manuel Ortega, the only Hispanic in my platoon. Ortega was from Austin, Texas. His parents were from Mexico City but Ortega was born in the States. He had grown used to the name calling and being looked down on for being Hispanic. We became very good friends during training when he saw there was no more respect for me than for himself. We came to see we were more alike than different.

Then there was Frances Gardner. He was a white guy who hated the name Frances, so we just called him Gardner. Gardner was from Long Beach, California and was big into surfing and anything to do with the beach or water.

The other guys in training teased Gardner about looking and sounding like characters in the beach party movies in the '60s. The Drill Instructor had taken to disliking him for some reason. He called Gardner "Surfer Guy" in a demeaning tone. Maybe he thought Gardner wasn't smart enough to be a SEAL, but I thought he might be hiding his intelligence; after all, his father was an attorney and pretty well off. He was sure born for the water. Later on he taught me to surf.

Gardner did not like the idea of me being called Shadow and Ortega being called a wetback. So we found common ground and respect for each other. Garner, Ortega and I became close friends.

We became a team within the Team. SEALs were supposed to pair off into swim buddies. You had to have your buddy's back at all times, know where he was at all times. Gardner, Ortega and I were unofficially a three-man group of swim buddies. They gave me nonstop encouragement. In turn, I encouraged them and motivated them every now and then.

Whenever either one of us felt like giving up and ringing the large brass bell, we would keep each other motivated. This would stop us from bailing out and kept us going. In our short journey, we helped each other any way we could.

There were plenty of reasons for needing encouragement thanks to the other crewmates. The worst was Gunner. He was from Vicksburg, Mississippi, and he bragged about coming from a long line of Confederate soldiers. He would often talk about the Ku Klux Klan and the importance of keeping the white race pure. "Just one drop of Black blood would make you a Black man," he liked to say.

Gunner was about 5' 11" and weighed the same as me, 175. He had this very heavy thick southern accent and I could hardly understand him half the time.

His buddy Combs was from Possum Creek, Tennessee, a small strip mining coal town that was as backwards as you could get. He was another not-so well to do southern gentleman, and I do use the term loosely. One afternoon during some down time us recruits were watching the news on TV, and there was Combs' grandmother lying on the ground in front of a bulldozer, protesting the strip mining in her town. Combs went nuts and requested time out of training to go home. His request was denied.

Gunner and Combs were usually accompanied by Duffield, who hailed from somewhere in Ohio. He was big, about 6' 2", and extraordinarily strong. He was a generally nasty guy who did not have a pleasant word for anyone.

CHAPTER 11
HISTORY LESSON

It was around this time that I started to watch the news on TV about the things more frequently being done to black people down South: being attacked by dogs and beaten by police, or having fire hoses turned on them. The song "Strange Fruit" by Billie Holiday told the story of Black people being hung from poplar trees down south. At times as an adult I helplessly watched the fight for freedom on the television.

I had been relatively unconcerned about race relations prior to entering the Navy. For example, everyone knows about Rosa Parks, but few people (myself included) knew the name Claudette Colvin. In March of 1955 she was a fifteen-year-old Black school girl in Montgomery, Alabama who refused to give up her bus seat to a white man. This was nine months before Rosa Parks did the same thing, but because Colvin was a minor the forces against segregation did not think she would make a good figurehead.

After the Rosa Parks incident, Martin Luther King, Jr. — relatively new to being a community leader — was asked to take on the Montgomery bus boycott. The boycott lasted for 385 days, during which time King was arrested and jailed. This helped catapult him into the national spotlight and during the 50s and 60s he became the figurehead of the American civil rights movement.

This movement was founded on non-violent measures, including sit-ins, marches, demonstrations and boycotts throughout the southern states. Throughout the years King made an effort to reign in any factions that could have promoted violence. But by openly violating laws they sought to fight, the protesters subjected themselves to violent attacks from the white establishment, such as police dogs and high pressure water hoses.

On August 28, 1963, Martin Luther King, Jr. stood on the steps of the Lincoln Memorial and delivered his famous "I have a dream" speech in front of more than a quarter of a million people of various races.

I was 15 and in high school at the time. I really did not know much about Dr. King or the fight for the right to vote. Nor did I know anything about Black nationalism, a movement born out of the hardships of Jim Crow laws down South.

In contrast to King's non-violent tendencies was Malcolm X, the public face of the Nation of Islam (a Black nationalist political/religious organization preaching Black self-reliance). He became one of the organization's most influential leaders, advocating for Black power and the separation of the races, and publicly criticizing Dr. King and the civil rights movement.

In the 1960s he renounced the Nation of Islam after the organization started to work more closely with civil rights organizations and religious groups. After leaving the Nation of Islam, Malcolm X was embraced by the Sunni faith and converted. During a 1964 pilgrimage to Mecca he saw Muslims of all colors interacting as equals, and realized that Islam could be the means to overcome racism.

Back in America Malcolm X faced death threats from the Nation of Islam, who now saw him as a hypocrite. He was murdered on February 21, 1965 by members of the Nation.

CHAPTER 12
HELL WEEK

There was a part of training that involved us being in a war type simulation. Our superiors would set up an entire base and act like the enemy. Even though we all knew it was just our superiors, the exercise was something that made a lot of people quit. This was called Hell Week, a time where we would be tortured and our loyalties would be measured. Our will to be in the SEALs was also tested. To this day, Hell Week is when Navy SEAL recruits see the largest drop off in every class. So many crew members surrender and ring the fabled brass bell that denotes giving up.

We were given no heads up as to when Hell Week would begin. It was a big secret, and every one of us expected it to happen on different dates. One night at 2 a.m., when we were all dozing in our beds, half dead from the day's training, a loud siren rang out. All of my crewmates began yelling and screaming.

"Hurry, get out of your racks and get dressed!" one commander ordered.

"We're being attacked!" said another one.

Due to the commotion, everyone was wide awake within seconds. Hell Week had officially begun.

We underwent five and a half days of continuous rigorous training. We had to run obstacle courses, conduct live fire evolutions, swim during the night in freezing water, and carry rafts over rocks during the nights. That latter task is called portage, typically done when carrying a raft across land from one body of water to another.

We were allowed no time to sleep, not even naps. My body felt numb and ached due to lack of rest but we just had to keep going until the end of Hell Week.

We played in the mud day and night, just covered with the stuff. We endured live fire and cover smoke while crawling under barbed wire. We carried logs and boats, on and off, up and down, nonstop with the instructors shouting at us, trying to beat us down mentally as well as physically to weed out the weak. Heavy spotlights flashed on and off, loud sounds of machine gun fire accompanied our evolutions, making sure we weren't given the chance to catch any sleep. We did get chow four times a day, but some recruits took the opportunity to nap instead.

The instructors kept yelling at me, "Get going Shadow, why don't you just quit? You are not worth the effort and time the Navy is putting into you."

We ran evolutions with a raft sitting on top of our heads. We ran almost 200 miles during Hell Week. We spent evolutions in a pool and in San Diego harbor wearing wet suits and fins. Those were some of the hardest times because the harbor water was so cold. The water temperature was between 55 and 69 degrees and we were kept in the water for hours upon hours, day and night, getting used to the frigid conditions. As a SEAL we would have to be able to withstand drastic situations, including ridiculously cold water.

Just thinking about what we were doing got harder and harder with all the grueling work and all the distractions. Each day there was no time to think about the next. I just wanted to get through one day at a time.

My two buds, Gardner and Ortega, stayed close to me. Ortega and I especially bore the brunt of constant nasty remarks. Instructors continually called me Shadow and him wetback.

At times my thoughts were to give up. Was this all worth it? The injustice at home, the disrespect in the Navy, what the hell was I trying to prove and to whom? Plus my father did not believe in me and my uncle thought I was mentally deficient for wanting to do this.

But I had to fight off my doubts. I had to prove things to myself and my family. And I had to prove to my instructors and my crewmates that I was just as good as them, regardless of the color of my skin. Giving up was not an option.

When Hell Week came to an end it was as if God Himself came down and said, "Well done, my son, well done." I had outlasted many white men to survive the ordeal.

Hell Week was designed in part to bring teammates closer together. Needless to say, however, nothing changed between me and Gunner, Combs or Duffield.

After catching up on sleep, Gardner, Ortega, and I tried to go out for drinks at a local bar to celebrate. But we forgot we were all too young to get in.

The author in Vietnam

CHAPTER 13
TRAINING
CONTINUES

After we completed BUD/S successfully, the next step was jump school: paratroopers. The Navy, unlike the other armed forces services, now runs its own jump school. But back then the Navy did not have a jump school so we used the Army's in Fort Bragg, North Carolina.

We started out learning how to jump and how to land, and then went on to learn how to put a chute on and how to maneuver with it. The T10 parachute weights 31 pounds and we would also have to pack and carry ammunition, weapons, food and sometimes web gear.

The first type of jump was a static line jump. That's where you attach your ripcord to a line in the airplane, and when you jump the chute is automatically deployed. Then we went to freefall jumping, which is when you pull the ripcord yourself. Timing was crucial.

Jump school was three weeks long. The fun didn't stop there. Next stop: SERE training (Survival, Evasion, Resistance, Escape).

SERE training was a particularly grueling time for all of us, as we would be taught what to do if we were captured while in action.

At the beginning of SERE training we were shown a charter that contained the naval code of conduct:

Article I. I am an American fighting in the force which guards my country and my life.

Article II. I will never surrender of my own free will. If in command, I will never surrender the members of my command.

Article III. If I am captured, I will continue to resist by all means available. I will make every effort to escape and to aid others to escape. I will accept neither parole nor special favor from the enemy.

Article IV. If I become a prisoner of war, I will refrain from sharing any personal information with fellow prisoners. I will give no information or take part in any action which might be harmful to my comrades.

Article V. Should I become a prisoner of war, I am required to give my name, rank, service number, and date of birth. I will evade further questioning to the best of my ability. I will make no oral or written statements disloyal to my country and its allies or harmful to their cause.

Article VI. I will never forget that I am an American fighting for freedom, taking responsibility for my actions, and being dedicated to the principles that made my country free. I will trust in my God and the United States of America.

SERE Training took place at the Marine Corps base camp in Pendleton, California. We also traveled to the swamps of Louisiana and the jungles of Panama to study jungle warfare. Most of the time we spent dragging our feet through the thick, slushy mud. Sometimes it would rain to the point where it would feel as if the forest was going to fill up with rain water and boil over.

We had started as a class of one hundred and sixty-five recruits, but only ninety-five found themselves making it to SERE Training. The number of people left would seemingly go down by one more every day. At every point in this phase I felt like it would be my own last day.

When we got to the base, we spent a week studying how

to live off the land and how to evade the enemy. After the classroom work was done, we were shown to a large, wooded field. We were let go in increments and were told to evade the enemy. It was an open field so there was nowhere to hide. Any hiding places that did exist were too obvious and the enemy already knew about them. It was like being left out to die, but we had to do the best we could.

We tried to camouflage ourselves, but everything that we tried was vastly inefficient. We spent a night out in the woods. It was dark, damp and quiet. Any sound made could be heard throughout the area, so we had to try to be as quiet as possible. The sounds of animals and insects would plague our minds the entire night, but even the slightest shift of the body produced a rustle of leaves or grass which could be very dangerous. We were all starving and there wasn't much food available. We had to eat whatever edible things we could find in the forest, but the land had been picked clean by the other classes that had gone through before us. Yet we still searched the best we could.

After that, we were to spend two weeks in a mock prisoner of war camp. We got the first look at the POW camp as we approached the gates. There were fences about nine or ten feet high covered with barbed wire. On the corners were guard towers and guards were posted with machine guns. Huge bright spotlights surrounded the camp, illuminating the area. Flying over the camp was a communist North Vietnamese flag and there was Asian music playing on loudspeakers which could be heard throughout the camp. All the guards had Vietnamese scarves on their faces and were wearing communist uniforms.

We were then taken to large dugouts in the ground, holes about eight feet deep with shallow wooden walls. These dugouts were topped with corrugated steel roofs and were divided into chambers. This is where our Team was supposed to sleep. Since the entire Team could not sleep in one chamber, Ortega, Gardner and I slept in one cave area. Gunner, Duffield and Combs slept in another.

That was day one. While this was a less than ideal situation, sleeping here was better than in the woods.

On day two, we were taken in groups to be interrogated. Interrogations took place in large shipping containers. On each container was some sort of writing which we assumed was Vietnamese. The guard told chamber one that since we could not read Vietnamese, we could not tell what the numbers were. When we were asked about them, if we got it wrong, he would slap us to the ground. Sometimes, I can still sense the hard, calloused and heavy hand striking my cheek. I got my fair share of bruises here.

The cargo containers were filled with very bright lights. They would make you stand with your hands tied behind your back and the lights forced into your face, blinding you. They would ask our name, rank, service number, what our mission was in Vietnam, who our commanding officer was, where our base was and how many others were with me. I would tell the interrogators, "My name is Watts, John O.; my rank engineman first class; service number 1190722; United States Navy." They would ask me this over and over and over again.

Then they would start in with, "You are a Black man. Why are you trying to fight us? You already have a fight at home. You have no freedom at home. Don't you know your mother is prostituting herself on the corners of Philadelphia? That's right, and your father is putting your mother out on the street because he can't find a job. They need the money to live. Your girlfriend is doing the same thing. She's sleeping with your friends just to make money. Why do you allow yourself to be degraded in such a manner? Come fight for us, fight with us and provide us the information that we need to defeat these white devils."

I would then again give my name, rank and service number in the branch of service. This torture went on all day long. Sometimes I would remember these lines in my head at night as I tried to drift off to sleep. But every time I closed my eyes, the words "Black man" seemed to flash in neon letters behind my closed eyelids.

When I finally got out of that cargo container, it was night. I went back to our hole in the ground where we were served what I thought was dinner. We got one meal a day and that was after dark. It was some kind of cold, slimy crap with chunks of meat and other things. This gooey textured food slowly slid down the back of your throat. They gave it to us in a tin cup. This went on for several days.

Living with PTSD now, the nights I spent in the hole are particularly prominent in my memory. This is probably because after an entire day of suffering and torture inside the cargo container, I went back to a dark, damp hole in the ground with barely any food or warmth to give me comfort. Sometimes I still dream that I fall from a metal bar into the hole that never ends; I keep falling, screaming into the void, until the voice in my throat dies out completely.

Next day, we were forced to get up before the sun and weren't allowed to rest until long after the sun went down. Every day we woke to a loudspeaker blaring communist music and propaganda. We were directed to stand in front of our cave, as I called it, so they could count to see if anyone had escaped during the night. We were made to stand at attention while they raised the communist flag.

Sometimes we had to bust boulders into big rocks. We would line the front of our cave with the rocks and paint them white.

The corrugated steel roof made it unbearably hot inside our cave, so we didn't spend much time in there during the day. If we weren't in the cargo containers being interrogated, we were on the other side of the camp in what was called the tiger cages. These were bamboo cages where you couldn't stand up, you couldn't stretch out or lay down, and you had to be on your hands and knees all day. If they thought you were falling asleep, they would come by and bang on the cage and ask you the same questions that they asked in the other type of interrogation.

If you were not in the bamboo cages, you were laid down on the ground and covered with a wool blanket. They would then stake the blanket down and soak it with water. This made it really heavy and it became extremely hard to move or breathe. It felt like a weight being pressed down upon your lungs, forcing all the air out so that you couldn't speak. Yet they continued to ask you the same types of questions. Sometimes the suffocation would make me dizzy and I would stop responding for a few seconds. This would result in a kick to the stomach or a slap to my already bruised face.

The guards and the interrogators were always trying to sow division within our team. At roll call in the morning, the interrogators would accuse one of the team members of divulging sensitive information. The interrogator would walk up and down in front of our line talking about information that was given to them, information that they could only know if one of us had talked; trying to turn us against one another, trying to break us.

One time the interrogator walked over to me and told me to step out of the line. He showed me to a nice table in the yard. Then the guard brought out a nice big breakfast which consisted of eggs, sausage, potatoes, toast and coffee. The mere sight of any proper food, let alone a big, finely cooked platter of it, made my mouth water immediately and I hoped this was some kind of reward for good performance.

Then the interrogator told everybody, "This is how we reward cooperation." He gestured for me to eat.

At that point, Gunner and Duffield said, "Wouldn't you know, it was that Nigger, Shadow. Of course he talked to the interrogators and gave them information about who our team is and what our mission was." I never even touched the food, of course.

Over those two weeks, POW camp training felt extremely real. Due to all the torture, everything we were put through and the entire atmosphere that was created, all of us became delusional and started believing that it wasn't just training, it was actually happening. We would frequently have people going nuts, believing that "the war was lost" when in fact it was just a simulation.

One morning we woke up and the American flag had replaced the North Vietnamese communist flag. The American Anthem played. This was a signal that the exercise was finally over. However, it was certainly not an end to the hardships that were to come.

The author's karate group in Vietnam

CHAPTER 14
HOME FOR CHRISTMAS

It was December 1966 and the team's training was over for the most part. Our duty assignment was the *U.S.S. Okinawa* LPH 3 (a landing craft helicopter platform).The *Okinawa* was a helicopter carrier that had Bell Cobra gunships and Cobra H-1 helicopters, nicknamed Hueys. All the Hueys were packed on the hangar deck. These copters were crucial for the war in Vietnam, as it was the first time in American warfare that troop movements were done primarily by helicopter.

Before our deployment, we were all given liberty and we all took our leave to go home for Christmas. After I arrived home, I spent two great weeks with my family, knowing that this time would soon enough come to an end and I would have to go back to full time duty. But at the same time, I was excited to put all of the training that I'd been through over the last year into action. In the back of my mind, I was looking forward to going to Vietnam.

I suppose there is some level of addiction in hardship. Once you get out of a miserable situation like the one we had found ourselves in, you feel like you need to prove yourself by getting through a bigger degree of hardship. That, mixed with the desire to utilize all that I had learned, was driving me to go to Vietnam.

The *U.S.S. Okinawa* had just finished refitting in Boston's

Navy shipyard. The entire team was supposed to report there on January 5, 1967. The ship was to go out for a three month shakedown cruise and the team would participate in war games in the Caribbean.

But as I boarded the ship, I received new orders that the ship was going to go to Vietnam and it was going to be away for a year. We were all then given another two weeks' leave and I went back home for that period of time.

When I got home, it was about 2 in the morning and everyone was asleep. My mom heard me coming into the house and she came to the top of the stairs to see who was coming in.

She yelled at me, "John, is that you? What are you doing home?"

"I'm home for another two weeks."

My mom came downstairs, angry and very upset. Tearing up, she said, "Boy, you are leaving to go to Vietnam, aren't you?"

"Yes, ma'am."

She slapped me across the face and started crying and begging me, her voice shaking, "Please come home to me. Come home safe." Then she spun around and walked away, turning her head as if nothing had just happened.

I wanted to stop her and tell her that I would come home. I wanted to hug her and reassure her. I even felt like I shouldn't go and risk my life. But I had to. I signed up for this.

CHAPTER 15
HISTORY LESSON

The first SEALs were sent to Vietnam in January of 1962 as advisors, to teach commando tactics to the South Vietnamese. Much of the SEAL units found themselves under CIA control until the end of 1963, when control was shifted to the standard branches of the American military. SEAL missions were usually controlled by Navy, Army, or Marine command.

SEAL involvement in Vietnam happened quickly. Today, SEAL training takes about a year. But during Vietnam, many SEALs went straight from BUD/S training to Vietnam in a span of months.

The first SEALs wore green Marine Corps uniforms or camouflage, but later denim pants became common because they did not make noise when they got wet and a man's legs rubbed together.

SEALs loaded themselves up with weapons and ammunition when they went out on patrol. They carried as much as they could, not knowing how long they'd be away from camp. Each SEAL was a one-man fighting force on his own. As a team, these platoons were the greatest soldiers alive.

SEALs also began using helicopters for missions, as Vietnam represented a new form of warfare which stressed the importance of using copters to move troops.

The author in Vietnam

CHAPTER 16
FIRST
DEPLOYMENT

Around mid-January 1967, the team returned to the *U.S.S. Okinawa* LPH 3 in Boston. The ship was preparing to get underway for a year's deployment in Vietnam. A year is a long time but I had no choice. I was kind of excited for the first mission, but at the same time I was scared because of my mother's reaction. I wanted to return home safe at all costs.

<u>Sailing West</u>

I met up with the team and we boarded the ship. After getting settled, the team was introduced to our new lieutenant, Gordon Maxwell. We called him L-T for short. He would be leading our team. After meeting with the lieutenant, we went to the tactical office. We were told that the ship was going to sail to Coronado, California to pick up the 5th Marine Division. This was because SEAL Team One and the 5th Marine Division would be conducting operations off the coast of South Vietnam. The ship would sail through the Panama Canal and then head up the coast of California to reach Coronado. Although we were only going from one part of the United States to another, it was still a long journey. We were told that we would be at sea for two weeks.

Since we were preparing for war, we had to ensure that all our weapons and gear were in working order. My team worked on stowing our gear and checking our weapons. We could not risk having faulty gear and weapons that didn't work. Checking equipment is one of the most crucial things for the Navy as well as any army in the world.

Two weeks at sea feels like ages. There was not a lot to do during this time. We worked out on the hangar deck wherever we could find room and I practiced my martial arts at the same time. We had to be in fighting shape. We also had to keep our gear and weapons in perfect condition so we continued to clean and break down our guns just to make sure that they were always in working order.

While aboard the ship, we did not have too much interaction with the other sailors. We stayed to ourselves mostly and avoided any conversation with others in order to hide our identities. They were not supposed to know who we were, what we were going to be doing, or who we reported to. It was like being undercover. We were on a mission and we could not risk any information getting out or falling into the wrong hands.

All the regular seamen aboard the Okinawa wore bell bottom jeans and denim long sleeve shirts. But the SEALs dressed differently. Our uniforms were jungle green or tiger stripes, no insignia, nothing identifying us as a black ops or special operations group, just our name tags. We were referred to only as a Naval special warfare group.

The sailors aboard the ship would give us weird looks and were curious about us. They always asked us about our outfits and why we dressed so differently from them. We never really answered them because we could not risk anyone knowing our true identities, as it could put our mission at risk.

As I said before, we were in SEAL Team One. It should have been like a family but it wasn't. It did not even feel like a team. There was so much tension between all of us. It was palpable and you could sense how strong it was if you walked into a room with all of us. If it wasn't for the two friends that I had on the Team, it would have been so much harder for me. Although I had made friends, I still had enemies: Gunner, Duffield and Combs.

Occasionally, our families would send us care packages. My mom would send me cakes in metal tins, along with other tasty treats such as cupcakes, potato chips, pretzels; all kinds of food that I liked. These care packages were like a reminder of home. After not having proper food for so long, these treats tasted heavenly. We would share what we got with our teammates, but the only two that wanted to share with me were my two friends, Ortega and Gardner. Nobody ever wanted to share with Combs because the care package his family would send him would have something called mountain oysters. These were hog balls in brine. Even if Combs liked me and was my friend, never in a million ears would I ever eat those slimy things.

Sailing the Pacific

Sailing through the Panama Canal was an amazing experience. We would sail into a lock, then they would fill the lock with water and you would feel the boat rise up. Then we would continue sailing forward. It felt almost like being on a ride at a carnival.

There were lush green jungles on either side of the canal. We could see tall, shady trees with vines hanging from their branches. The crowns of the trees were full of leaves. Our journey continued through the canal with this calming scenery.

Amazingly, it took us two weeks to get through the Panama Canal. After our passage, we were awarded a certificate called "the order of the locks," just to show that we went through the Canal.

When we arrived in Coronado we docked and prepared to be joined by the 5th Marine Division. Since we had done our

SEAL training in Coronado, it was nice going back there. We had only a limited time, though, a quick stop before our long journey. There was no time for leisure and we could only admire Coronado from afar.

Many of the Marines that we were with had never worked with a Black SEAL before, as there weren't many Black people who wanted to be in the SEALs. But the Marines were a great group of guys and they had no problem working with me while most of my own team avoided me. When the Marines noticed that my team was not very cooperative with me, they couldn't understand what the problem was.

They asked, if I was capable and cooperative, why did my mates avoid me? Why did most of my own team not include me? Why did they call me Shadow? When I told them it was because I was Black and that some team members had started rumors during training, it did not sit very well with them. They thought that it was unjustified and it was hard for them to believe the extent to which some people would go.

While the ship was getting ready to start on a long trek across the Pacific to Vietnam, we took on fuel, food and mail. We could only load up the necessities in the short time we had.

The Okinawa pulled out of San Diego harbor and finally headed for the open ocean. Once we got beyond breakwater, the speed of the ship increased to 30 knots (34 mph). Most Navy ships sail in a straight line, but the Okinawa did not. The ship constantly went in and out as if in a zigzag pattern. This was a maneuver to prevent being attacked by another ship just in case we encountered enemy craft on our way through the Pacific. It would be hard for another ship to aim when their target was constantly changing its course.

After two and a half weeks at sea, the ship pulled into Honolulu, Hawaii. The team was granted an eight hour day pass to explore a little bit, as we had been confined to the ship for what felt like ages and needed a change of surroundings.

After refueling, we left directly for the coast of Vietnam. Everyone started feeling an adrenaline rush. This was it. We were finally going to our first war. This is what we all had trained for.

We were at sea for several weeks on our way to Vietnam, specifically the coast of Da Nang. Being at sea at night is very relaxing and peaceful. Looking out over the ocean, it appears as black as a velvet curtain. It feels haunting, yet somewhat calms the soul at the same time. The stars are so bright, they illuminate the dark sky. There are a lot more stars in the sky over the sea than there are over land because there are not many city lights to interfere or air pollution to cover the stars.

Being on this long voyage gave me way too much time to think about my family and friends. Worrying about the possibility that you may never see loved ones again or even hear their voices really keeps a young man's mind occupied while away. It also saddens the heart that you might not be able to say one last goodbye. It's bad enough to ponder not being able to fulfill all your dreams and aspirations if you don't make it back from war, but thinking of what people close to you would go through is even worse. They are just left at home, anxious, awaiting our return. If we don't make it, it destroys them.

I think if someone is aged and sick, their death is easier to accept. But being in the Army or Navy, or any force that fights and risks death, that's a choice you make. An intentional choice to risk taking yourself away from your loved ones. I thought of my mother and how she disapproved of my decision to come to Vietnam. I had left her distraught. I think that is how everyone's close relatives felt.

Arrival in Asia

We finally arrived off the coast of South Vietnam. We

could see the shoreline of Da Nang in the distance and the lights of the city. We were finally there.

We could also hear explosions and saw flashes of lights. My heart was nearly pounding out of my chest because we were at war. I had imagined being here but arriving made it all too real.

Hunters, trackers and interpreters
who worked with the Team

CHAPTER 17
FIRST FIREFIGHT

The following day the team had to wake up at 0400 hours. We assembled in the tactical room with some of the Marines to plan out the mission for the following day. We were to go right to work. No more breaks for us.

Our mission was to work with the Marines as a long range reconnaissance unit. The brass had received intelligence that the North Vietnamese Army (the NVA) was planning to outflank the Army and the Marines that were stationed on a hill designated Hill 811. My team and the Marines were to be out beyond the wire tracking the movements of the NVA along with the Viet Cong.

The Viet Cong were guerrilla fighters from South Vietnam who were allied with the Communist Northern Vietnamese Army. The name Viet Cong was shorthand for the Vietnamese term for Vietnamese Communist. Our troops also referred to them as Victor Charlie, or just Charlie, for the letters the American forces used as a phonetic alphabet (Alpha, Bravo, Charlie, Delta, etc.).

There would be a total of seven Navy SEALs and six Marine Force recons on our assignment. We all got together to plan out a strategy.

When the time came to act, we geared up and boarded a Huey H-1 helicopter and were taken to Hill 811 north. Another unit was working Hill 811 south. The Marine division took to the flight deck and loaded up the Huey H-1. We were set to back up the Marines on the hill when the chopper touched down on the landing zone.

The weather was very hot and dry. I already felt dehydrated and I was scared. I found myself praying to God to let me get through this day. What I did not know at the moment was that this day would not end in a mere twenty-four hours. It was going to last two weeks.

The first day seemed endless and began a period where I no longer comprehended the concept of time. We were out beyond the wire several days at a time. While we were out, we looked for trails and hiding holes for the Viet Cong. We did not have a lot of ground cover and Hill 811 was barren, so we couldn't conduct a lot of movement during the day. Most of our movement was during the night so we could sneak around without being seen.

Killing the enemy was not part of this mission. We were instructed that our primary job was to gather intelligence including, if we could, capturing a North Vietnamese Army soldier.

The whole purpose of going out in the night was to not be seen and we had to be as quiet as possible so we didn't end up alerting the NVA. We could not fire our weapons for fear of giving away our position. I wasn't really concerned about our weapons giving us away, I was more concerned about the sound of my heart. I was so nervous, although only I could hear it, it felt like everyone around me could tell how loudly my heart was beating.

This was our first mission and we had spent about two weeks preparing aboard the Okinawa for it. We ate a lot of dried rice, fish, and lots of roasted vegetables, typical Vietnamese fare, so when we took dumps our feces wouldn't give away the fact that Americans were in the area. We hadn't taken showers in several days. We weren't even allowed a wash up as we didn't want our American body odor to give us away while we were hiding.

It finally began. We were told to lay low and stay as still as humanly possible. The Viet Cong started moving forward with the NVA behind. We were lying in the tall grass and we had to stay perfectly quiet as to not give away our positions. While we lay in the grass, bugs of all kinds crawled over us. Mosquitoes and bees would bite us and buzz in our ears. No matter how irritating it was or how much our bodies itched, we had to control ourselves. No involuntary actions such as scratching ourselves and swatting away the bugs. We had to lay as still as statues. I could feel the sweat trickling down my back.

While we were in hiding, a Marine lookout popped a sun flare. The night sky lit up like high noon and then everything was illuminated. We could see that the enemy forces were sneaking up on the area. It looked to be 500 or more NVA and Viet Cong. I was scared at being surrounded, knowing that even the tiniest movement could cost me my life. I just lay there, limp, turning all my energy inward in order to not move a muscle.

From where we were in the tall grass, we could hear the alarm being sounded back at base camp. That meant we couldn't stay in that position any longer. So we went back the way we had come, trying to avoid any Viet Cong or NVA soldiers. But since there were so many of us and it is easy to spot moving grass, that wish was short lived.

We found ourselves in a major firefight. This was the first firefight I had ever been in and it felt surreal. I'm sure all of us were afraid for our lives. We all felt like we were going to die. I was so anxious in that moment, I was shaking.

Even though we were scared, we had to be ready to fight. But since we knew that the Marines were going to be hitting the area with mortars and artillery fire, we had to dig in and stay as close to the ground as we could to avoid getting shot. More flares popped up, and the more the flares went up, the more enemy soldiers we saw.

My heart was pounding even more than it had been before. As loud as it felt, I thought like everyone around me could tell where I was. Either the beating of my heart would give up my position, or I would somehow mess up and get shot. I just knew I was going to die. But this was what I signed up for, so I had to man up, stop thinking negatively and just do what I had to do even if I didn't want to.

With a dry throat, feeling dehydrated, and the sunlight pricking my eyes and skin, I fought. The battle was fierce and it went on for days.

The Marines were lobbing in mortars and the 105 MM and the M 102 Howitzers. At one point I heard nearby gunshots and my heart jumped. One of the Marines had taken a round to the head. When I saw the man flat on the ground, I felt my heart stop. The loud sound of the guns being fired was already making me jumpy, and now seeing one of the Marines lying limp on the ground made me wish (not for the first time) that I wasn't there. We approached him to see if he could be helped, but he was out and down for the count. We didn't have the ability to do anything for him. All we could do was fight for our own lives.

Although we were a team, it felt like every man for himself in that moment. But SEALs and Marines never leave a man behind. We had to find a way to get the fallen Marine back to base.

Someone back at the base called in an airstrike with napalm. A few minutes later, jets flew overhead and the airstrike was dropped on the enemy. The smell of napalm is something you can never forget, a powerful chemical that fills the air. That and the smell of the enemy's burning flesh was everywhere.

There were hundreds of dead Viet Cong and NVA all over the field. Even though it was a battleground and they were the dead bodies of the enemy, it was an image that I could never forget. That sight still haunts my soul.

Finally, there was a retreat. The enemy started backing up as fast as they had come. They were gone within minutes.

This went on for days and the days turned into weeks. The Marines took very heavy casualties and the medevac choppers were in and out all day and into the night. Whenever we saw a medevac chopper, we would know that a Marine had been injured or killed. This would always send a wave of sadness through me.

After two weeks, our SEAL team was pulled out and returned to the *U.S.S. Okinawa*. When I got off the chopper, it was like something out of a nightmare. The crew was hosing off the choppers and the decks were covered in blood. It was everywhere, like seeing a river of red flowing through the surfaces on the *Okinawa*. Body bags were piling up on the flight deck and the hangar deck. I had never seen anything like it, so many dead bodies at once. It sent a chill down my spine.

The wounded Marines that had been brought back were then moved to the *U.S.S. Sanctuary*, a hospital ship.

This had been our first firefight. My knees were still shaking, my hands shaking, my entire body was shaking. I had to exert all my energy to appear still. Sweat was dripping off my brow, not from the heat but from high anxiety due to the situation we had just been in: a near death experience. And just our first.

When the team got off the chopper, we went below decks to the tactical room where we were debriefed. After the debriefing we went to our quarters and showered for the first time in ages.

We then tended to our weapons. Everything had to be broken down, cleaned and reassembled so it would be ready for the next mission, whenever that would be.

Gunner piped up with a mean grin. "Hey, Shadow Nigger did okay."

Combs replied, "Yeah, even broken clocks are right twice a day."

Subic Bay

After another week on the ship, off the coast of South Vietnam, we were told that we were going to leave and head for the Philippine Islands. Our next port of call was going to be a place called Subic Bay. Other sailors aboard the ship who had previously been to Subic Bay told us that they called it Shit City.

After getting there we found out why. A steel bridge crossed over a sewage ditch with all the waste from all over the city. This waste flowed underneath the bridge and it smelled horrible.

But Subic Bay was the place where sailors would end up for rest and relaxation after being on the line in South Vietnam for more than 30 days. This was a chance to wind down from all that we had experienced. The city was loaded with bars, women, night clubs and any kind of debauchery you could think of. That was the wildest and the craziest time I've ever spent in my entire life.

We would meet women, get drunk and have a good time. I am not much of a drinker because I don't like the idea of not being in control of my actions and forgetting things. I always wanted to have the right head for thinking and making logical decisions, especially being the only "shadow" on the SEAL team. I was always at a point of hyper vigilance, always knowing my surroundings, so I didn't drink much.

One day I met a woman in a bar in Subic Bay. Her name was Erlinda Solomon and she was a native Filipino. She was beautiful: 18 years old, hair as black as ravens' wings with dark eyes to match, and caramel colored skin. We really hit it off and she became my steady girlfriend whenever I was in port. I would always end up meeting with her whenever I was there. We also started writing to each other when I was out to sea.

The ship pulled out of Subic Bay to return to the line in South Vietnam. While we were out to sea we would work out on the hangar deck. Sometimes I would practice my karate breaking skills by using terracotta roofing shingles, breaking ten to twelve at time.

Gunner was feeling a little nasty towards me, but this was nothing new. He said to me, "Let's see just how good you really are, Watts."

"What do you mean?" I asked.

"Let's spar."

"How?"

"Well, you're so great," Gunner said. "How about I use my Ka-Bar." He held up his large Navy service knife. "And you can use just your hands."

Gunner came at me, slashing and lunging. I felt like he was truly trying to hurt me.

Our lieutenant saw what was going on and put a stop to it. "If you're going to spar with a knife," he told Gunner, "put a Goddamn sheath on the Ka-Bar or use a practice knife."

Gunner sheathed his Ka-Bar. He came at me again, slashing and stabbing. I moved to one side and let his motion carry him past me. As he moved past, I hit him with a backhand strike. He stumbled, almost hitting the deck. As he regained his balance, I lashed out with my right leg in a crescent kick to his right wrist, knocking the knife from his hand. I spun and aimed a back heel kick to his jaw. You could hear the impact from yards away. The impact knocked him out before he even hit the ground.

Our lieutenant stepped in at that point to put a stop to the match, but it was already over. Gunner was lying flat on his back on the deck, his buddies racing over to check on him. I turned and calmly walked away. No pats on the back for me.

The author in Vietnam

CHAPTER 18
MEN WITH
GREEN FACES

The Viet Cong called us *kguon dan ong voi khoun mat xanh,*which means men with green faces. We wore very heavy dark green camouflage face paint that made us harder to see during the day and almost impossible to see at night. Some of the guys had on a blend of colors, black as well as green, to give them more of a leafy look. When we were in the jungle on patrol our dark green faces helped keep us unseen by the Viet Cong. There were times when the team would be just a few feet from Viet Cong soldiers but they could not see us. We were good enough to gather intelligence, sneak into an enemy camp, take a prisoner, and slip away … all without being seen or heard.

At night the dark green face paint would look black. Gunner would say to me, "You don't need the camo, you are dark enough." I would get hellbent mad but would not say anything, for fear of getting shot in the back from one of my own. That was not an unheard of custom among superior officers who tended to put their own men in the line of fire; I didn't want to suffer that same fate.

The Viet Cong were interred along the Perfume River, sometimes laying water mines for Navy patrol boats on patrol. At times we were tasked with rooting these enemy forces out, traveling upriver in our rubber boat known as a Zodiac, or Zod for short. We would lie close to the gunnels, where the sides met the deck, keeping a low profile to the water, and the outboard motor was baffled to keep the nose level as low as possible. We would often come under small arms fire, but thanks be to God the VC were usually bad shots.

One time the team was on a sneak and peek mission to count and report back on enemy troops. I was on point with Ortega to my right and Gardner to the left, forming "the tip of the spear." It was a cold and rainy day, and the Viet Cong had been using a game trail, so it was hard to follow them in the mud.

The jungle had a heavy smell of decaying vegetation. The tree canopy was very dense, blocking out any stars and making the night even darker. Our interpreter requested we slow down because he had heard something ahead in the bush.

The noise became louder and more intense. I held up a fist to direct the Team to stop and we all took a knee and waited.

It turned out to be a tusker, a very big boar. It had been rooting through the ground, looking for food, when it sprung a punji stick trap: sharpened wooden sticks standing upright in a hole covered over with brush to keep it hidden. The sticks were covered with the enemy's shit so you would get blood poisoning if you stepped on them.

The boar fell into the trap and the spikes ripped through its body. We could hear it thrashing and wailing from the pit. It was only by God's grace that the boar fell into the punji stick trap, because the pit had been in my line of travel and I could have easily missed it.

If the creature wasn't fatally wounded then, it would die eventually. The Viet Cong smeared their shit on the spikes to give their victims blood poisoning on the off chance the spikes didn't do the job right away. I remembered that when I was 10 years old I saw a movie called *China Gate* that dealt with French Foreign Legion mercenaries fighting in the First Indochina War. Nat King Cole was fighting at the Battle of

Dien Bien Phu when he stepped on a spike trap. He survived, only to die later in the movie from his wounds.

We were about a week into this search and had not spotted any Viet Cong. After another day we started seeing tracks that had been made from short pieces of tire rubber. The VC wore homemade sandals that incorporated pieces of tire rubber as the soles, so we knew the enemy was close.

After a while we spotted the Viet Cong traveling in a long line, carrying bags of rice and ammunition plus ChiComm (Chinese Communist) AK-47 rifles towards an underground tunnel. We silently counted; there were over 300 of the enemy soldiers.

The team fell back and we radioed the coordinates to HQ, then quickly cleared the area and waited. Air Force planes flew over and carpet bombed the area.

Afterwards our Team had to go back and determine how effective the air strike had been, including counting the dead and seeing if the weapons stash had been hit. The air strike had been on point. Another mission accomplished by our little unit.

Men with green faces

CHAPTER 19
OPERATION
BEAR CLAW

The *Okinawa* was back on the line in South Vietnam, and we were preparing for Operation Bear Claw. This was a search and capture mission, north above the place called Hue but below the DMZ (the demilitarized zone between North and South Vietnam). After a few days of prep, we were ready to start the operation.

It was after midnight when we boarded the copters. The door gunner sat on one side with his 50-caliber machine gun, and some of the team sat with their legs hanging out the other side. We wore camouflage in a pattern like tiger stripes, and our faces were similarly painted green and black.

Combs was cracking off, repeating his "joke" that I did not need the black paint because I was already Black. Being the brunt of their jokes made me truly angry because I felt I had already proven myself in combat, but I had to stay in control.

When the chopper hovered over our landing area, we rappelled down ropes dangling from the helicopter, about 50 feet into a deep green abyss. It was after midnight and black as pitch when we descended on our ropes. When we hit the ground, we all took a knee in a semicircle, weapons at the ready, looking out over the jungle.

The lieutenant took out his topographical map and plotted a course. We steered clear of any villages or locals that were in the area. As we moved through the jungle, I was assigned to walk point. I hated that position. I had to look out for booby traps, tripwires, and Viet Cong hidden in the jungle.

As I moved through the jungle in point position, if I came across something suspicious I would make a fist and raise it high. The team would stop and the lieutenant or the platoon leader would come forward to see what I was looking at.

Later the next day we came across a patrol of NVA and Viet Cong, about fifty enemy soldiers. We were spotted and a firefight broke out. We took cover in the jungle behind trees and earthen formations.

The team spotted a tunnel that the Viet Cong must have used for hiding. It was too small for all of us to fit into, so we blew the tunnel with a satchel charge.

The fighting went on for several hours. We were pinned down, seven of us against fifty, but we were SEALs so the fight was even.

Eventually we were stuck at a standstill. We had to fight back and save the mission at any cost, there was no choice, so we called in for air support. Once the Huey gunship came the tide turned and we beat the enemy back.

It was such a thrilling experience. Although we knew that we were risking our lives, there was an unknown excitement within us.

The operation continued for some time. Finally, on day twelve, we were given a special mission: to capture an NVA officer. On day 15, after night had fallen, we spotted an NVA camp.

I remember that feeling of joy I felt, a feeling that seemed to be shared among my teammates; we had hope inside our hearts that we would definitely be able to accomplish our mission. The key was to approach it as smartly and silently as we could.

We worked our way closer to the camp's tree line.

Everything was still and quiet. There were only two NVA sentries posted. The lieutenant sent two of the Team to dispatch the sentries with no noise, each sentry ending up the recipient of a Ka-Bar slicing across their throats. That was basically half the mission there: getting in undetected. The only chance of success was to take the camp by surprise. We didn't want to give even the slightest hint of our presence.

We moved further into the camp as silently as possible. One of the team had located an NVA officer. As soon as we stepped inside the camp, the NVA soldiers spotted us and began to load their weapons. There was a sudden mess in the camp as they tried their best to attack us, but it was already too late for them.

We immediately began killing the NVA soldiers, making sure not to hurt the officer. The enemy dug in, using their small huts for cover. Gunfire lit up the night, back and forth. We worked our way through the camp until the last enemy soldier had been downed. None of our team was injured. Two of our men took the NVA officer prisoner, tying him up and gagging him.

The team scooped up papers, maps, anything that could provide intelligence, and hightailed it back to base with our prisoner in tow. Mission accomplished, no men lost.

Navy Meritorious Unit Commendation

Navy Unit Commendation

Combat Action Ribbon

CHAPTER 20
HISTORY LESSON

SEALs were typically tasked with intelligence gathering, finding and capturing enemy soldiers, and locating and rescuing prisoner of war camps. Teams One and Two were assigned to patrol beaches and waterways, performing guerilla assignments like destroying munitions and killing enemy leaders.

There were nearly 400 active SEALs in Vietnam, although no more than 120 (from both Team One and Team Two) at any one time.

Surfing during Vietnam

CHAPTER 21
VISITING
HONG KONG

After sixty days we returned to the ship for some much needed rest and relaxation and left Vietnam for Hong Kong. We anchored in the city's harbor. Just like everybody else, we were told that Hong Kong was a shoppers' paradise.

I was especially interested in fashion, and learned that I could literally have any type of clothing prepared for me in less than a day. I found a *GQ* magazine and cut out pictures of Nehru suits because I wanted the same designs for myself. I remember going on shore leave and finding a tailor shop where I ordered two Nehru suits and several shirts for myself. One suit was a gray silk sharkskin, the other was black silk; they were both very glamorous and trendy.

The tailor took care of even the smallest details that I conveyed to him. All of the shirts had my initials monogrammed on the pocket and on the sleeves of the French cuffs. I also ordered a camel hair overcoat for myself, which turned out to be amazing!! I just loved the texture and wore it several times after my journey.

We only stayed in Hong Kong for a few days, so we didn't have a lot of time to explore the whole city. Still, we all loved our stay there as it was a very nice and cozy place.

Although the trip was super short, I tried to discover some of the cafes and restaurants. I wanted to try their best foods. I remember eating several times at the Jumbo Kingdom

Floating Restaurant in the Hong Kong Harbor. I just fell in love with their food, it was really scrumptious. I also took the tram to Victoria Peak, which I absolutely enjoyed.

After returning to the ship, we set sail for South Vietnam again. Shortly after boarding, a surprise inspection took place. Lieutenant Maxwell entered our cabin and inspected our living quarters. Everything was going peacefully up till that point, but then I suddenly raised my mattress to check everything and ended up finding a .50-caliber round underneath! It was more than shocking to me. I just could not believe what had happened and wondered where it had come from.

"You want to explain this, Watts?" the Lieutenant asked.

"L-T, I swear, I have no idea how that got there. You know how careful I am with my weapons. This must have been planted by somebody else."

But it was no use; he considered me at fault. Lieutenant Maxwell wrote me up for improper storage of ammunition and I had to go to captain's mass, which is where the captain or the Team leaders decide on disciplinary actions.

All that time, I was just praying to the Lord to make things better for me and get me out of trouble. I was angry and disappointed at the same time. I clearly knew who planted the ammunition, I knew that it had to be all Gunner's doing; he intentionally planted the bullet under my mattress to be found during the inspection. But of course I could not mention his name as I did not have any evidence. I knew if I went to the lieutenant with no proof, it would look like I was trying to lay the blame on someone else. So I decided to behave like a real man and face the ongoing misery with full confidence. And as much as I did not like it, I had to have these guys continue to watch my back, just as I watched theirs. I knew Gunner was not beyond actually shooting me in the back.

Unfortunately, my rank was reduced by one grade, and I was also denied a good conduct medal that I had been due. I got my rank back eventually but never did get that medal.

CHAPTER 22

BACK TO
VIETNAM

Operation Bear Claw was still underway when the ship got back on the line in South Vietnam. The team spent the next few days preparing for our next mission.

One night, two Marines came up to me below decks, which was a very secluded part of the ship. They straight away asked me, "Can you break bones as easily as you break roofing tiles?"

I just replied to them with a simple, "Yes, I can."

Nervously, one of the men said, "Can you break our legs for us?"

"What?"

"Please. That way we won't be able to go back out on the next mission."

I could see the fear in their eyes and hear the pleading in their voices. As much as I wanted to help them, I just could not do it. I had an extreme fear inside me that if this act got out and the authorities found out what had really happened, I would end up being court-martialed and imprisoned. So I did not do anything to them at all.

The Team started preparing to go back out. While we were in the gear room, packing up, Duffield asked me how it felt to go to captain's mass. He told me, "I bet you will know how to store ammo now, won't you?" with a big grin on his face, then laughed loudly. I felt like kicking him in the balls as hard as I could, but of course I could do no such thing.

Our next mission was to be conducted on the border between Vietnam and Laos. The chopper ride from the ship was a little over an hour. We hovered over the landing zone and jumped out. The ground was soft and muddy because it had rained the previous day. I kept on thinking, This could be my time to die. Even though I knew that it was not very positive or optimistic of me to think that way, I just could not help myself.

We all made our weapons ready. We moved forward in single file as always, and I took point. The jungle was very thick; you could hardly see the stars at night or the sun during the day. It was full of bushes and enormous trees that covered every inch of the forest. It was all green everywhere you looked.

Due to the excessive vegetation and climate, we had to move at a very slow speed. I came across a series of punji stick traps. I alerted the team and motioned for them to move around the traps.

The CIA was looking for confirmation that the Viet Cong and NVA were using the crossing between Vietnam and Laos to move further south into South Vietnam. We were almost a week into the mission before we spotted any enemy forces. Imagine a week of nothing but slowly treading through the bush, on alert at all times, and nothing happening. It was enough to wear a man down mentally.

All of a sudden, our little band was looking down at several hundred Viet Cong and NVA. This mission was supposed to be all sneak and peek; there was no action involved up till then, and I was fine with keeping it that way. We did not let our presence be known, slipping away from the enemy troops and continuing our scouting operation.

We spotted more Viet Cong and NVA every day. This proved to us that the enemy was already on the move.

The Team was hidden in thick vegetation. With our green tiger stripe camo and our faces painted green we were almost invisible. At one point we were less than ten feet from the enemy, as still as stones, when an NVA soldier stopped and looked our way. He started walking in our direction.

No one moved.

He got to the tree line and came into the jungle about two feet, then stopped. I was on point as usual, so I was the closest one to the NVA soldier. I slowly drew my 7-inch Ka-Bar knife from its sheath, ready to silently dispatch him. Then he pulled down his pants, squatted, and took a dump.

Just as he was about to finish, he cocked his head as if listening to some sound. Again I readied to attack. Just then the NVA soldier reached behind himself, grabbed a handful of leaves, and wiped his nasty ass.

As we watched them walk by us we saw that the Viet Cong soldiers were carrying what looked to be 25 to 30 lb. bags of rice on their backs. The Team trailed the enemy force for several days, keeping tabs on where they were stashing their rice, guns, and ammunition. After reporting the situation we told command the enemy locations.

Command radioed back that we were to stop following the enemy and begin to fall back. They were calling in the big guns, and I mean the big guns: the AC-47 (Attack Cargo Gun Ship) with three 30-inch 7.62MM General Electric Miniguns, better known as Puff the Magic Dragon. The enemy called it the Dragon Ship. It would shoot a red flare round after every five regular 7.62 rounds. The rate of fire was 2,000 to 6,000 rounds per minute, so fast that all you could see was a line of red fire coming from the sky.

That night hellfire rained down on the Viet Cong and NVA. The sound was deafening. The volley came down for less than five minutes. When we went back to confirm the success of the attack it was like nothing I had ever seen. Men were cut in half, and some body parts were stuck to trees.

Mutilated corpses were strewn all over the ground.

After searching another two weeks, we could not find anything but locals and small fishing villages, so we were called back to the ship. The jungle was too thick for a chopper landing, so we had to use a tactic called Special Patrol Insertion/Extraction (SPIE). Each SEAL hooks on to a long rope on the chopper, which then flies out with us hanging underneath.

I could not wait to get back to the ship to take a nice long hot shower and eat some good food. I had steak on my mind.

Once aboard we immediately went to a debriefing in the tactical room. All mission details were relayed to command. Because I had been on point, I was asked whether I did something that could have alerted the enemy to our presence. Even though it was an unfair question, it was not unexpected.

CHAPTER 23
TIME IN THAILAND

Now it was time for the ship to weigh anchor for another port. This time it was Bangkok, Thailand. This was truly a place like no other. Up till then, I used to think that Subic Bay in the Philippines was the wildest place, but after the trip to Bangkok I profoundly changed my mind.

Thailand was indeed the most happening and exotic place that I had seen until that time in my life. All the bars and clubs were on two main streets, Sukhumvit Road and Khoa Sun Road. There were uncountable spots, all equally fancy and glamorous, so that it was impossible to pick the best of them.

You could see hot chicks roaming here and there, enjoying the best time of their lives, and DJs playing jazz. American Soul music blared from inside the clubs, music like James Brown, The Temptations, and the Supremes. All the clubs had nude strippers, which added to the charm of the night discos; they were ready to give you the best time of your life!

If you were looking for a girl for the night, a pimp would bring five or six girls for you to pick from—all of them charming and beautiful. You could pick just one or take them all; it was only $5 per girl! There were random dudes hitting up on chicks for the night, everything was super seductive—all those erotic strippers and dancers, the hot ambiance, and the exotic music working together to draw you in like a flute player hypnotizes a cobra. It was indeed a tremendous experience! So far, one of the best ones I'd ever had in my young years.

CHAPTER 24
LAST MISSION BEFORE STATESIDE

After leaving Bangkok, the *Okinawa* went back on the line in Vietnam for another month to take on more wounded. Body bags keep piling up on the hangar deck and the ship's refrigerators were getting full. It felt unnatural seeing all the bodies lying about. The ship in essence was becoming a floating morgue.

Any fun had gone out of everything. The ship's crew had slowed its talking and joking around, and the officers became stricter. Things that the officers used to let pass were now being written up.

Our Team got orders that we were going to a small village of the Hmong people located in the central highlands in South Vietnam. We were going to train some of the people in the village along with the Green Berets, who were Army Special Forces. The Hmong people were small in stature and very friendly and eager to learn to keep the Viet Cong from terrorizing their village. Our time in country—that is, just before the ship would pull out to return to the states—was to be three weeks.

The training was in the use of the M1 carbine: how to load and keep it clean, and more importantly how to shoot. How to shoot from standing position, while taking a knee, or lying on your belly. There was live fire training using heavy machine guns during simulated mortar fire to mirror shooting in a combat scenario.

We also trained the Hmong in the use of radio equipment and setting up radio networks; the use of grenades and satchel charges; how to build fortifications; how to man a sentry post and properly stand guard. We also tried to teach hand to hand combat skills.

The training was extremely hard, even with the use of an interpreter. Kids would come up to me and touch my skin to see if the darkness would rub off, or touch my hair because it felt different to them.

Duffield said, "We're not the only ones that think your blackness is strange."

I told him, "You're just jealous because they find me handsome and you just pale."

Duffield replied, "You want a piece of this pale man, come on, any time any place."

The lieutenant stepped in and shut it down quick. Duffield's last words to me were "Watch your back, Shadow; watch your back."

The whole time the villagers were looking at us, smiling, laughing and pointing. They were very friendly and easy to get along with and had no idea about the conflict between me and my so-called teammates.

The food during that period was not what I would call a fan favorite, even though it was fresh. The menu was a steady diet of dried fish rice, vegetables and boiled pork. As for me, I actually preferred my C-rations: canned pork and beans, and spaghetti with meat sauce.

The Team soon returned to the ship, and we were on our way back stateside with a short stop in Hawaii for food and fuel. Total sea time was three weeks. The ship docked in San Diego in mid-December, 1967. The team was granted two weeks leave and we all went home for Christmas.

It was great being home but all I wanted was some quiet

time, time to clear my head and try to forget the things I had witnessed over the last year. I had to get in the right frame of mind to prepare to go back for another year.

The author in Vietnam

CHAPTER 25

FINDING RELIGION

I had started going to church when I was about 8 years old. We were all raised Baptist, but not strictly so. I was baptized at 13; that's when the church believed you were old enough to know and accept God.

My brother and sisters and I would go to Wayland Temple Baptist Church on the corner of 25th and Columbia, sometimes with our parents, sometimes just us kids. Mom would give each of us a nickel to put into the collection plate. She would come with us fairly often, but Dad would only be there on special occasions.

Church services were very, very long and very, very boring. Church would start at 9:00 or 10:00 each Sunday morning and be over at 1:00 or 1:30 in the afternoon. I did not like going, but then what child likes sitting in a large hot building singing songs they do not understand?

I was also part of the church's Cub Scouts and Boy Scouts, so there was at least some fun associated with the church.

The church would hold Holy Communion once a month. The Communion "menu" included Welch's Grape Juice and unsalted crackers. One Saturday, after a Cub Scout meeting in the church basement, we found the Communion so-called wine and helped ourselves. All of us scouts sat and drank the juice until there was none left. When the Pastor went to set up the Communion table and found no juice left, he was angry beyond words. He had to send someone to the corner store to buy more juice. When the Pastor found that the Cub Scouts drank the juice, he banned the Scouts from the church. We had to have our meetings at the den mothers' houses.

As I got older, I started learning about preachers like Harlem's "Sweet Daddy" Grace and Father Divine (the latter of whom moved to Philly in his later years). I saw how they would take money from the poorest people to line their own pockets. "Sweet Daddy" Grace drove a Silver Phantom Rolls Royce while Father Divine lived in a gated mansion on Philadelphia's upscale Main Line.

After my childhood we left Wayland Temple Baptist Church and started going to a new church, Zion Baptist, helmed by Reverend Leon Sullivan. I attended Zion until I went to Vietnam.

While we served in Vietnam, a lot of the platoon members received correspondence from their respective churches. Most of the guys got cards saying things like, "We're praying for you." I got letters saying my dues were in arrears.

CHAPTER 26
SECOND TOUR
IN VIETNAM

It was mid-January 1968. The team had reported back to San Diego Naval Base. It was good seeing Gardner and Ortega but not so much with the other three: Gunner, Duffield and Combs. With that bunch, nothing had changed.

Gunner was a big talker, always bragging. He made sure to tell me about time over the holidays he spent with the KKK — that's right, he bragged to me about spending time with the Ku Klux Klan. He had told them there was a Nigger on his team and was supposedly advised to take me out if he had the chance; it would be better for the country and his own safety.

Gunner was a real piece of work. He was good at being a SEAL but bad at being a human being. I asked him, other than my skin color why did he dislike me so much? He said that he had been taught that Niggers came from apes, our brains were smaller, and we were cowards. There was no reasoning with him and no changing his mind, so I just let it go.

Combs and Duffield were simply his followers. Whatever Gunner had to say, they went along with it.

Our return flight to Vietnam was booked on a chartered jet, Tiger Airlines. The flight was fifteen hours long and each of us was a bundle of nerves. When the jet landed in Da Nang and I set foot on the ground, the sounds and smells all came back. It was like I had never left.

At that time, my mind said to my inner self, "What the hell are you doing coming back to this hellhole?

We were taken to our barracks at Da Nang Navy Base, where we unpacked and stowed our gear in our lockers. I went to take a dump and a shower, and there cleaning the latrine was an old Vietnamese woman (a *mama-san*). She was looking at my nakedness, smiling, showing her black betel nut teeth. I immediately covered myself with a towel and said to the old lady, "*Di Di*" which translates to "Go go."

The Next Mission

The next day we met up with our lieutenant. He informed us we were going to be assigned to an assault river boat crew. The boat was a MK2 PBR (Patrol Boat River), better known as a swift boat. The PBR has a top speed of 28.5 Knots (32 MPH). It held a crew of four and its armaments included twin .50 caliber machine guns in a rotation tub forward and a .60 caliber 7.62MM machine gun. We would be working the Perfume River, which is a busy thoroughfare for sampans (local boats) trying to smuggle contraband to the Viet Cong.

Ortega, Gardner and I took some time to explore the base. We were very surprised to find a full-size movie theater, a swimming pool and a bowling alley. The base definitely did not lack things to do. The food at the commissary was nothing short of phenomenal: eggs to order in the morning with pancakes, sausage, bacon, all kinds of foods for breakfast. For lunch there were all kind of sandwiches, and for dinner we could choose from steaks, chops, roast beef and pork.

After a few days off base we had been getting a little slack in our physical fitness routines, so it was back to the grinder working out. We also spent time on the shooting range.

Gunner and the others never let up with their taunting of me and Ortega. They still called me Shadow and Ortega a wetback, but we never let that break our spirits. At one point Ortega walked over to Gunner and told him, "You'll need us as a team before we need you."

We met our boat's four-man crew. Tom Abrams was the boat coxswain, the driver. The crew also included Jordan Parkes, James Wilmore, and Brian Law. The boat was very slick and had a 671-turbine jet drive.

As a team we had to prepare for a mission. This preparation made tracking and staying under the radar of the Viet Cong easier. We would stop taking showers that would otherwise mask our body odor, because we wanted to smell more like them. We started eating more food like the Viet Cong so our shit would not have peas and corn in it—telltale signs that Americans had been there.

After a few days of becoming familiar with the crew and the boat we left at midnight to go up the Perfume River, headed for the city named Hue. The river was a dark muddy brown with lots of garbage and silt floating about. There were several basket boats out on the river. We had to check to see whether they were actually casting their nets trying to catch fish, or planting small mines in the river to interrupt Navy LCUs (Landing Craft Utility) or other commerce moving up and down the river.

The PBR pulled into a small jetty on an island in the river and the team got out to look around. There was what appeared to be a dead Viet Cong soldier lying on the beach. The strangest thing happened to me: in my mind I could hear the dead man talking to me. He was begging me to help him get up so he could stand on his own two feet.

The dead man said, "Why are you just standing there? Help me. I am not dead, but I am so very cold. The sun is out but I can't feel its warmth. I know I am in water, but I can't feel it is wet. Hey, Black man, don't just stand there, help me."

Gardner touched my shoulder and asked, "Watts, are you okay?"

"Yeah, I'm okay. Just a little distracted, but on track now."

Once we returned to the river, we started taking small arms fire from holes that had been dug into the riverbank across the way. Gunner took the twin .50s and I grabbed the .60 on the tail. We chewed up a lot of mud and grass with our firepower. Someone's arm flopped out of a hole but that person was not moving.

Swift boats were fiberglass, made for speed, not for taking a lot of small arms fire. Abrams hit the throttle to get our asses out of there. James Wilmore took a direct hit in the chest, but luckily his flak jacket took most of the round. Still, he had a small wound.

The team was hunkered down in the belly of the boat trying to return fire over the wall of the gunwale. My .60 had a steel shield in front and the enemy rounds were pinging off of it like hail on a winter night. My mind was racing trying to home in on the shooter, but it was dark and Viet Cong did not use tracer rounds. I just sprayed the riverbank with as many 7.62 rounds as I could. There was no time to pray but God knew my heart.

Da Nang

By the grace of God, we made it to Hue and back to Da Nang with no other problems. Wilmore was taken to the hospital and turned out to be fine.

The rest of us took some time to look around the city. It was full of people, almost wall to wall. Most people rode bicycles. There were very few cars, and most of the autos were military vehicles.

Shops sold food of all Asian influences. It had the feel of a Chinatown, almost as cosmopolitan as Hong Kong had been. The girls and women wore black silk pants and white silk tops, with straw hats shaped like wide funnels. Children ran throughout the streets selling almost everything.

But as the old adage went, buyer beware. One of the favorite items for sale was whiskey, anything that came in a dark bottle like Jack Daniels or Jim Beam. The kids would steam the seals off the bottles, pour the whiskey into something else, pee in the bottles, then reseal them. Then some unsuspecting soldier would buy them for far less than what they would sell for back home.

If you looked closely, the city was not as nice underneath. The streets were dirty, and rats bravely darted in and out of sewers and walked on overhead electrical wires.

Da Nang is where we got our first look at the Korean soldiers known as ROK (Republic Of Korea) Marines. These guys were very hard core. They would keep track of their kills by wearing ears strung around their necks. I heard it said they were mercenaries and paid by the kill; hence the ears as trophies. The Korean Marines were big in stature and their hand-to-hand fighting skills were not to be taken lightly.

This is where I was introduced to taekwondo, a Korean equivalent to Shotokan Karate. I was intrigued with this fighting style and wanted to learn it. After some time observing the ROKs I found a Korean master working out at the base gym. His name was Kim Da Jung. I asked him to teach me, and he only agreed after I demonstrated my own skills (which were nothing in comparison to his). Every martial art is different, yet there is actually quite a lot of overlap when all is said and done. I found myself quite adept at certain aspects of taekwondo.

CHAPTER 27
THE BEGINNING OF TET

It was coming up on the end of January and the streets of Da Nang were crowded with people preparing for Tet, the lunar new year, the Vietnamese equivalent to the Chinese new year. We were told that a cease fire would be going into effect at 0800 the morning of January 27, 1968 between Army of the Republic of Vietnam troops and the communist Viet Cong. But within the throngs of southern Vietnamese were Viet Cong and NVA infiltrating the city, posing as regular people. We were to stay on high alert status for possible violations of the cease fire on both sides.

Our team was ordered north to Hue to reconnoiter Viet Cong movements. Our swift boat left Da Nang at 1300 on January 28, 1968. The river was very quiet, actually too quiet for my liking. The water was like glass, with no sampans or basket boats out fishing. It was all very odd, very eerie. The team was on edge and the hairs on the back of my own neck were standing up.

But much to our surprise we made it to Hue with no trouble. We docked at our destination, the Nguyen Hoang steel bridge that crossed the Perfume River.

In the early morning hours of January 31, 1968, a division-sized force of NVA and VC soldiers launched a coordinated attack on the city of Hue. They attacked the western wall of the Citadel, seeking to capture the Mang Ca garrison, the Tay Loc airfield and the Imperial Palace.

It was a massive mortar and artillery attack on Hue. Mortars struck the dock where our PBR was tied to the dock cleats. Gunner yelled, "Tom, get your crew and move the PBR!"

Tom Abrams, the coxswain, and the rest of his crew ran full tilt for the swift boat and managed to get aboard and start the engines. Just as the PBR was about to pull away from the dock, a mortar hit the boat dead on. We watched helplessly as the crew and the boat were tossed high into the air. All the rest of us could do was run with our heads down and try to find cover.

Marines moved to the Nguyen Hoang steel bridge to blow it so no enemy troops could approach Hue. The first attempt failed but the next one tore the bridge to shards of steel. This held back the Viet Cong onslaught for a short time.

It was too little too late, as thousands of Viet Cong were already in the city. We were taking fire from the buildings within Hue. South of the river a reinforced company of the enemy's 2nd Sapper battalion, thousands of soldiers, launched an attack on the Military Assistance Command Compound.

Hue was under siege from all sides by North Vietnam Army troops and Viet Cong. There were only about 200 U.S. Marines stationed in Hue, along with a smaller number of Australian troops, up against thousands of enemy combatants.

The Viet Cong were trained in jungle fighting, not urban combat; but for that matter, neither were we. It was a learn as you go type of deal. We went street to street, house to house, one at a time searching for the enemy.

As daybreak came the dust and rubble from bombed out buildings made the going hard. The fighting went one building at a time as we sought to clear out implanted VC and NVA troops. The enemy shelled the city relentlessly for hours. The dead and dying were all over the streets.

The U.S. Marines were tenacious and risked their all, as did our little SEAL Team. There was no safe haven, we were all just trying to stay alive.

Gardner entered a building and lobbed in a fragmentation grenade. After it went off he ran in shooting. He came out with a baby wrapped in a blanket. The rest of the team covered Gardner as he ran but he was clipped in the calf by enemy fire. Ortega went to him to help him get to cover. All along, Gardner kept the baby in his arms.

The Marines brought three M-48 Patton tanks up and started shelling the other side of the river. The Cong shelled us back. As much as we would throw at them, we got back in kind. The lieutenant had us move out to the main street of Hue — or what remained of the main street. Bodies littered the ground. Some of them were still burning.

We worked our way through the city. Gunner was firing on any person who made a move to try and shoot but I think he was having fun. He shouted at them all, "Dirty Gooks!"

After we found cover the lieutenant got in his face. "We need prisoners! We need information! Try to take some alive, dammit!"

Civilians ran through the streets, screaming and yelling, holding their children by the hands and often dragging them. Others carried bundles of belongings on their heads and under their arms, yelling, "Chay nhanh" or "Run fast."

The main street led to a building called the Citadel. At one time this had been the seat of the government. American and ARVN forces headed there for shelter because we were being overrun by the enemy.

Gardner still had the baby in his arms. I had come across an injured teenage girl and, without thinking, slung her over my back to carry her to safety. The girl had a sucking chest wound and she was bleeding badly but the fighting was so intense that there was no time to stop and drop off our passengers.

As we ran from one place of cover to the next the girl I was carrying took a stitch of enemy rounds up her back. As I laid her on the ground, I thanked God for saving my life and I thanked the girl also.

Duffield yelled, "See, Gooks are good for something. Too bad Shadow didn't get hit." Then he laughed.

The lieutenant addressed the Team, "Knock off the chatter and keep the racial shit to yourselves. Stay focused."

The shelling continued all day and into the night. Finding a place to hunker down was getting harder and harder. The Citadel was only one klick (a mile and half) down range. Archimedes said that the shortest distance between two points is a straight line, but that was not so in this case because of the bodies in the streets, destroyed buildings, and enemy shells falling. We ran hunched over, taking cover anywhere we could.

As we ran past one building we saw movement inside. We entered to check it out and found an old *mama-san*. She was pointing to the second floor to warn us of the presence of enemy troops. Gardner gave her the baby and the Team started up the stairs. I was walking point.

I got two steps up and a grenade bounced off the wall above and onto the steps in front of me. "Grenade!" I yelled, then jumped over the railing to the floor below, covering my head with my hands. The *mama-san* with the baby ran out the front door as a hail of rounds rang out from above us. It tore up the wall while the Team was kissing the floor. We returned fire and lobbed several fragmentation grenades up the stairs. After the shooting stopped we headed up, only to find two dead NVA in a sniper's nest. One had been the sniper and the other his spotter.

Ammo was running low. They were trying to get a supply drop from HQ in Da Nang, but HQ was being hit hard. The captain at HQ told our lieutenant that it had been a coordinated attack throughout all South Vietnam and it would be hard getting a resupply chopper out to us. As NVA shelling continued, our lieutenant relayed what was going on. "This is all part of a coordinated attack. HQ doesn't know if they can get us a resupply. We have to conserve our ammo. It could be several days before we could be replenished."

Gunner with his smart mouth said, "When we run out of ammo what are we supposed to do? Throw rocks at them?"

The lieutenant replied, "If we have to, yes, throw rocks. We are SEALs, dammit, not some whining pussies. We're SEALs! So suck it up. The order is to shoot when you see a body and not before."

As we pulled out of our cover spot three NVA charged us. One came directly at me with a knife in his hand. I stood my ground as he slashed his blade back and forth in the air. I backed up but kept my hands off my guns. He was yelling something in Vietnamese and his eyes were hot with hatred. I had not seen the enemy this close — alive — before. The NVA soldier switched his style and came in with a downward stab. I came forward and caught his wrist, moved to the side, and drove the knife into his stomach. It tore the man from one side to the other and his intestines spilled out. As the man fell I moved away and felt something squish under my boot. I had stepped on his insides as they dropped to the ground.

All along we could see the Citadel in the distance. It looked like a Chinese castle with a moat all the way around it. Bronze Chinese temple dogs sat in front of the gate, one on each side. It took the better part of two days just to go one and a half miles to get to it.

We ran at double time through the streets until we finally made it to the Citadel. We felt safe for the moment and took very long and deep breaths for the first time. The Citadel was packed with civilians, a lot of women and children.

We took stock of what we had. Food and ammunition were low, and the attacks of the Viet Cong were continuing, so we had to ration what little supplies we had as the siege of Hue continued.

The NVA were rooting out city leaders and shooting them in the streets. Our Team, along with some Marines, was sent out to try to find as many city officials as possible. Each group was sent out with an interpreter to explain our mission and read the street signs so we would know where we were going. We were assigned to search Le Loi, a street along the Perfume River that goes straight into downtown Hue. We found mass graves of what we believed to be city officials and their families. The bodies had been covered with lye to help them decompose more quickly.

The Viet Cong were still in temporary control of the city and we ran into a number of small firefights, but it appeared that the NVA and Viet Cong were pulling back. We returned to the Citadel and reported what we had seen.

We finally got an air drop of supplies. Better late than never.

As the NVA and Viet Cong withdrew, skirmishes were diminishing. We were assigned to take part in the mopping up of Hue, going house to house to clean up and take the city back one building at a time. We encountered very large numbers of Viet Cong who surrendered to us.

We went almost four weeks with no showers, no changes of clothes, no brushing of teeth; we all felt nasty. We were all very, very ripe.

The Team got a chopper back to Da Nang. It was the first week of March. Gardner got his leg attended to, but it was only a scratch so they just gave him a large Band Aid. We all laughed, telling him, "No Purple Heart for you, buddy. That's not going to get you sent home either." Not that Gardner wanted to go home; none of us SEALs were quitters.

We went to a debriefing where we learned that Tet had been part of a coordinated attack by the Northern Vietnamese

Army and Viet Cong that had taken place throughout all of South Vietnam. Their promised cease fire for the new year had been a false flag because they knew that most of the ARVN soldiers had been sent home on leave and therefore were unable to respond to the attack. The fighting during Tet had reached Da Nang and that city was a mess, but not as bad as Hue. Buildings were bombed out but the bodies had already been removed from the streets when we got there.

The author in a PBR

CHAPTER 28
BOATING IS NOT MY FORTE

It was good being back at base. A hot shower and a full night's sleep felt soooo very good.

Gunner started in on Ortega during his shower, saying, "Don't forget to get your back wet. He's a wetback, get it? Wet back." He and his buddies were the only ones laughing, of course.

The next few days were quiet. Gardner, Ortega and I went to China Beach, a local place in Da Nang with a nice sandy beach for relaxing. We took some brewskies and settled down for some much-needed quiet time. But the break did not last long because we were scheduled to be sent back out on the river on another patrol boat.

We spent a few days getting our gear together and refilling our clips with ammunition. The next day we loaded everything on the new boat and headed out on the Perfume River at 0300.

The PBR cruised upriver at low speed to reduce noise. The only sounds were insects and monkeys chittering in the jungle. We went with no running lights and it was pitch black. We were on a kill and capture mission to locate NVA troops and take their officers prisoner. At least, capture who we could and kill those we could not take alive.

The river was smooth and very quiet. My mind was still on the action in Hue after Tet. I continued to pray that God would help me to stay focused and still my fearful nerves. I asked Jesus to protect my team and to turn us into a brotherhood, all of us looking out for each other.

As the sun came up over the jungle the night mist lifted. There was a light fog in the air and the smell of fresh cut grass. Villagers started to stir, and fishermen were putting their sampans in the river for a day of fishing.

A kid in a dugout boat was motioning if he could come alongside. He was not threatening. The bottom of his boat was covered with pitch and his paddle was just a piece of board. The PBR slowed so the kid could float up next to us and he simply asked for something to eat. We gave him some of our C-rations. Combs said, "Don't feed that little Gook, that dumb motherfucker. He wants to be our friend during the day then he'll try to kill us at night."

Duffield yelled, "Someone just shoot the motherfucker!"

But I was trying to make a friend, so I asked the kid if I could try out his boat. He gave me the okay sign.

I stepped over onto his boat, sat down, took his homemade oar and started paddling. What I did not realize was that I was letting more water into the boat than I was putting back into the river. The back of the boat started sinking and I foolishly tried to hold the boat up with my feet under the cross bar in the middle. The boat slowly sank to the bottom of the river.

I got reported to command. My pay was docked, and a new boat was bought for the boy. He was the only kid on the river with an aluminum canoe.

I believe that that eventually got him killed. We found the canoe in the river one day, with his body laying inside it, shot up.

As the days and week went on there we experienced one skirmish after another. We tracked the enemy, taking NVA and Viet Cong officers as prisoners.

CHAPTER 29
NEWS FROM HOME

The news from home was not fun. The racial tension in America was only getting worse. There were riots in the streets, with people setting fires to stores and protesting against the Vietnam war. It sounded very bad. And Hanoi Hannah, the voice of Northern Vietnamese radio who tried to turn American soldiers to their cause, took full advantage of the unrest in the States. Hanoi Hannah would speak out directly to Black soldiers, telling us how our families were being treated at home. Black people were losing their jobs everywhere. They were routinely being beaten by police and jailed. Whether she was telling the truth or not, her words only made a hard time harder and a bad time worse.

And then we got the word that on April 4, 1968, Dr. Martin Luther King, Jr. had been assassinated. Gunner said at that moment, "It was just a matter of time before someone shot that Nigger."

Well, I lost it. I did not see a fellow Team member, all I could see was a white racist pig and I could not take it any longer. I gave him a lunging side kick to his stomach and he went down.

When he got back up, he came charging at me, yelling and cursing. "All right, Nigger, I am going to kick your Black ass."

I took a fighting stance and, as he ran toward me, I threw

out a foot and swept his legs from under him. On his way back up I dropped a downward elbow to the top of his head. I figured that was enough, and started walking away.

Gunner got up and grabbed me, saying, "Don't turn your back on me, Nigger!"

At that point I grabbed his hand and twisted his wrist into a joint lock, then tugged downward so he lost his footing and hit the ground again.

Duffield and Combs wanted to get into it, but the lieutenant showed up. "What the hell is going on here? Who started this mess?"

Gunner and I looked at each other. Gunner surprised me when he said, "We were practicing hand to hand fighting, L-T."

The lieutenant replied, "That's a load of shit. If I find you two practicing hand to hand like this again, someone is going to get written up."

This was not an isolated incident. Similar occurrences were happening throughout Vietnam. Blacks and whites were fighting each other over the assassination of Dr. King.

Back Home

In the middle of April the American Red Cross notified my commander that I had a family emergency: my grandmother had passed away. I requested two weeks to go home to attend her funeral.

Maryum Watts had been an integral part of my growing up. My grandmother always had a kind and encouraging word for me. No matter what others would say about me, she would tell me there was nothing I could not do if I put my mind to it.

When my mom and I found time to talk during my two weeks back home she asked me, "What the hell did they do to my baby over there? There is a sadness and anger in your eyes that was not there before. What do they have you doing?

Tell me what happened to you."

I could not tell her what my eyes had seen or the things my hands had done. I just smiled the best I could and told her, "I'll be okay. It's just going to take some time."

The rest of my time at home was quiet, spending most of my time alone except for going to an uncle's bachelor party. I had trouble fitting in, though. Trouble getting back to the old John Watts who had left for Vietnam.

I also took a girl out on a blind date. Her name was Patricia Ford. I liked her, but we did not hit it off. She said I had too much of the war in me and she did not like that. She thought I was an angry young man who was ready to fight at the drop of a hat. I was not capable of polite conversation and did not have any kind words, just the nasty mouth of a SEAL who had just left a war zone.

While home in Philadelphia I witnessed a further decline in race relations, especially under then-police commissioner Frank Rizzo. Rizzo had been a hard and brutal policeman, and as commissioner he was known for his racist views and hard stance on Black neighborhoods. I was often stopped by the police while in uniform, and they requested to see my papers granting me leave. This was to see if I was AWOL (absent without leave). It was just another form of harassment.

The death of Martin Luther King, Jr. hit the Black community very hard. He was a man who had inspired many with his uplifting words. But for me his nonviolent protests led to men and women being beaten in the streets by police, having dogs sicced on them, and fire hoses turned on full force. I hated seeing the footage on TV. It made me think, Why I am fighting in a war halfway around the world for a country that treats its people like that?

CHAPTER 30

BACK ON
THE MARCH

A few days later I found myself back in Vietnam. I found that nothing had changed between Gunner and me. He still had it out for me.

Our next mission was to locate a POW camp in the jungle that had been spotted by an aerial reconnaissance flyover. There were several American soldiers and a downed chopper pilot that we were directed to bring back.

We entered the river above Hue in our swift boat. The jungle was very dense in that part of the country. The PBR pulled into a small inlet, then we covered the boat with a camouflage net. The boat crew would hang tight and wait there for four days. If we did not return in time, they had orders to go back to Da Nang without us.

We walked in single file, seven to eight feet between each of us. Each man had his M16 at the ready. This part of the country had more than just Viet Cong and NVA to worry about; there were big Asian tigers roaming free in the jungle. At night you could hear them roaring. We all slept close to each other, no fire allowed for warmth because it would signal our presence. One man stood watch at all times.

After three days the POW camp was spotted. There was no fence, just a single guard in front of the camp. We expected to see at least six American prisoners but there was only one in sight: the chopper pilot, tied up and left out in the open.

We decided to make our move after midnight. I was to take point once again. I moved slowly and softly toward the camp. As I came up behind the guard I saw that he was smaller and shorter than me. With my Ka-Bar knife in my right hand I grabbed the guard from behind, throwing my left hand over his mouth.

The guard was taken totally by surprise. He grabbed at my hand and wrist, fighting to break loose of my grip. I rammed the Ka-Bar into the base of his neck, jamming it into his brain. I wiggled it around to scramble the brain and cut the brain stem from the spine.

The rest of the team flooded in to take out the remaining guards. A firefight broke out with the rest of the enemy soldiers in the camp. Combs ran into the camp and headed straight for the pilot. He cut the man's bindings and pulled him to his feet, then dragged him to safety.

We found the camp officer and took him as the only prisoner. Gunner radioed headquarters to tell them what had happened and requested that the PBR wait for us on site for another two days. We headed back without incident and met up with the boat, with our downed pilot and a prisoner in hand.

Surf's Up

We spent some time back in Da Nang between missions. The living was good. Gardner's father had somehow found a way to send him a 7-foot surfboard; I think it was a Banana or a Skag. He started teaching me how to surf in the enlisted persons' pool. Learning to surf was fun. I was looking forward to getting good enough that I could take a board to China Beach and catch a wave there.

I also found a way to improve my fighting skills. At the base gym there was a new Korean taekwondo teacher by the name of Jeong Hoon. He was the master of the class, or Sabonim (instructor). I learned much more from him than the previous taekwondo instructor I had met. Shotokan Japanese Karate and taekwondo were very similar, which made learning easy. After six months of intense training, I earned a black belt in that discipline.

While training with Master Hoon I met several South Korean Republic of Korea Marines. They were very focused and determined warriors. I saw them do things as martial artists I had never seen before. My skills compared to theirs were minuscule.

I would later learn that our team would be going on capture or kill missions with some of these ROK Marines. When the time came, I felt comfortable working with the ROKs. My team of five was joined by four ROKs.

The ROKs would hear Gunner and Duffield calling me Shadow, and under their breath sometimes Nigger. They did not understand the term, and one of the ROKs asked me about it. I told him that some whites in the U.S. think African Americans were less than them — inferior.

One mission took us southeast along the Cambodian border into the Central Highlands of Vietnam, where the people known as Montagnards resided. Green Berets had been training the indigenous Montagnards in jungle warfare. They were expert trackers and hunters and their hatred of the Viet Cong made them great allies.

Our team and the ROKs took two Montagnards with us to help track the Viet Cong. The Montagnards pursued the enemy for two days, taking us high into the mountains. The jungle was very thick, which made the going hard.

We came across a village that the Viet Cong had raided. They had killed most of the men and raped the woman. The men had been killed because they refused to help the Viet Cong.

On the third day we caught up with the Viet Cong patrol. The VC had taken about twenty Montagnards, conscripting them to act as forced labor and to fight for the north. We followed the Viet Cong patrol until nightfall, waiting for the right time to attack.

After everyone settled down for the night the ROKs took out the guards. The Montagnards homed in on the captives who had been taken by force. Our team took up flanking positions and opened up on the rest of the Viet Cong in the camp. The ROKs did the same.

Some of the Viet Cong threw down their weapons and surrendered, but the rest tried to fight us off. When the firefight was over the ROKs cut off an ear from each dead Viet Cong soldier. This was the first time I had ever seen the act done in person. We took the Viet Cong prisoners back to Da nang for interrogation.

Promotion

Before our break was over I received a promotion to E5 Engineman. Although I had not touched a diesel engine in over a year, diesel mechanic was still my official job classification. SEALs were still very classified so there was no special SEAL job classification at that time.

My compensation increased from our $278 a month base pay because we got an extra $55 hazardous duty pay each month we were in country. Our pay was not in U.S. dollars but in Military Payment Certificates. MPCs were used to keep the American dollar out of the hands of the Vietnamese. It was a different color, like Monopoly money. Every few months the color would change, and the Army, Navy, Marines, and Air Force would have to turn in their MPCs for a new color.

All good things must come to an end, and the team received new orders: to go back to Hue and search out and destroy. This mission included the capture of high ranked city officials and infiltrated enemy soldiers who had helped with the attack on Hue.

Our PBR hit the river full throttle with the diesel turbine

blasting water through the jet pump. We reached top speeds of 28 knots, or 32 mph. The twin guns on the bow and the single .50 caliber that was aft were manned at all times.

We made it to Hue without a single shot fired (by us or at us). After we pulled up to the dock, several Vietnamese kids came running to the boat and started begging for food. Supplies in Hue had been very low after the attack on the city.

Gunner started cursing and screaming at the kids. "You fuckin' Gooks! Can't you just die? I hate you fucking Gooks."

I turned to Gunner and said, "Stop cursing, would you? They're just kids. They're just hungry."

"They are Gooks just like you are a Nigger," he replied, "so why don't you shut your fucking Nigger mouth."

It seemed that Gunner was never going to give me—or anyone else—a break, no matter what I said or did.

There was a Landing Craft Utility (LCU) also tied to the dock. The Team went on board and below decks to get some rest. Later that night, while everyone else was asleep, I went over to Gunner's rack and took one of his socks out of his boots. I returned to my rack and masturbated in his sock, then snuck back and put the sock back in his boot. The next morning when Gunner got up he put his socks on. One was all stuck together and full of cum.

He was mad as hell, yelling, "What the fuck is this shit in my sock?"

The lieutenant told him, "You should know better than to take your boots and socks off while on high alert."

We all had a good laugh at his stupidity.

CHAPTER 31

HOT AIR

The Team hit the streets armed with CIA intelligence, which in my humble opinion wasn't worth two good shits. There were a lot of Marines also working the streets. We moved toward the city center looking for city officials. Our interpreter asked every civilian we encountered if they had seen any city officials, but we were told mostly the same thing by everyone: the city officials had fled the city with the NVA and Viet Cong. They pointed across the river, which we could not cross without our PBR.

We searched the city for several hours to no avail. Finally we called it a day, and headed back to the PBR to take it up the river.

It was nightfall before we got to the other side of the river to start our search anew. There were multiple trails through the dense forest, and traces from the Viet Cong retreat all over the place, so it was impossible to know which trail we should take.

The night was as black as ink, and the tree canopies were very dense, blocking the moonlight and the stars. Gardner walked point because he had a Starlight night vision ocular scope mounted on his M16. He used it to help the team through the jungle. The going was very slow because we had to make sure not to trip any booby traps.

The jungle was full of night cries, the sounds sometimes

making my mind wander. But we also used the chattering of monkeys to help hide our own footsteps from the enemy.

Time passed slowly as we hunted. We had to move even slower in the darkness.

Gardner raised his left hand into a fist, signaling the team to stop. Everyone took a knee.

Gardner signaled for the lieutenant to come forward. He said there was an NVA unit camped directly ahead.

We were vastly outnumbered so we did not engage. We stayed as low as possible and carefully moved back the way we had come. After we were about one klick away the lieutenant called for "hot air" on the enemy's position: napalm. A jet soon streaked overhead and past us, dropping flaming death on the NVA encampment.

We had to wait for the napalm to cool down before we could approach. We counted 75 dead NVA soldiers, charred beyond recognition, twisted in different positions of anguish and horror.

Our search mission continued. No rest for the weary.

Next up to take point was Combs. It was getting on to daybreak and making our way through the jungle became a bit more manageable.

We encountered nothing for the next day and a half. Then we found a Viet Cong and NVA stronghold. It appeared to be inside a cave carved into the side of a mountain. Our radio was not working so we could not alert headquarters about our discovery. All we could do was count the number of NVA and Viet Cong soldiers and make note of the location for future reference.

On the way back to the river we ran into an enemy patrol, about 20 NVA soldiers. They spotted us and we started taking on heavy automatic weapons fire.

Ortega had an M79 rocket launcher. He fired it and lit their asses up. I lobbed some white phosphorus grenades at them.

Phosphorus is some nasty shit; like napalm it sticks to you, you can't just snuff it out like a normal flame. My grenades had the NVA and Viet Cong literally on fire, screaming and rolling on the ground trying to get the phosphorus off their bodies and clothes, but to no avail.

We returned fire in leapfrog fashion. Three SEALs would run toward the enemy while firing, then another three or four would do the same, crossing the ground between us as we went.

It was not a long firefight, just a few minutes. All told, we killed 14 enemy combatants. The others all ran away. We weren't inclined to pursue them, as we didn't know if they were headed for reinforcements or making their way through a booby-trapped area meant to take us out.

When our time was up for this particular mission we headed back to our PBR and took off downriver. We made our way back to Da Nang without any further incident.

Upon our return we all had to be debriefed. Command was told of the NVA and Viet Cong stronghold, and the very high number of enemy troops we had spotted.

After we cleaned our weapons and stowed our gear, we all got some hot chow and showers, then went to the infirmary to have any minor wounds attended. After that, it was time for a few days of rest.

First Class Petty Officer.
At the time SEAL was not
a classification so each member
of the team had a different job.
The author was an engineman.

CHAPTER 32

A GIRL DOWN UNDER

Gardner, Ortega and I went to downtown Da Nang to visit a brothel. There was nothing new inside, just the same girls as always. But as we were being entertained we heard a loud commotion coming from the street and rushed outside to see what the furor was about.

Sitting in the middle of the street was a Buddhist monk dressed in bright yellow. He held a can of gasoline and, as he was chanting, he poured the gas over his head. We watched in horror as he lit a match and set himself on fire. Not a scream came from his mouth, not a whimper or any indication he was in pain. He just sat their burning until he fell over dead.

I asked one of the locals, "What was that all about?"

"It is a protest against Catholicism."

"What? Why?"

"Your people are converting the Buddhist faithful away from the path of Buddha."

I didn't know anything about that, I was just stunned by the spectacle. It seemed like a senseless act of suicide. But I held my emotions in check; it was not like I had never seen a man burning before. Although this was the first time I had seen a man set himself on fire.

We were off mission for two weeks. They showed movies

on base for us and we saw *2001: A Space Odyssey*. A very strange movie.

Gardner, Ortega and I took some time to go into town to see a musical show. There were groups of Filipinos who would come in-country and entertain our troops. The shows were very cool, they would sing soul music like James Brown, The Temptations, and the Supremes. They also played American style country and western music.

The entire Team was then granted one week of R&R. This meant a full week off of combat patrols. We could go anywhere we wanted, except we could not go back to the States past Hawaii.

I chose to explore Sydney, Australia. After landing in Sydney, I made my way to the local U.S.O. (the United Services Organizations, civilians who entertain the troops). Staffers included young ladies who volunteered to show soldiers around the city.

I was assigned to a very nice young white woman named Rachel Sanborn. She even took me to meet her parents at their home. Rachel's mother, Mrs. Sanborn, made me a great seafood dinner of shrimp and fried grouper. It was the best food I'd had in almost a year.

Rachel took me around Sydney. I saw the Sydney opera house and all the night clubs I could have asked for.

Mrs. Sanborn asked me to call home to the U.S. so she could talk to my mother. She asked my mom what my favorite meal was so she could make it for me! I loved roasted leg of lamb with mint jelly, collard greens and biscuits. Mrs. Sanders had everything she needed to make this very special dinner except for the greens, but I wasn't complaining. For my last dinner in Sydney, it was amazing.

At the end of my R&R I prepared myself mentally to head back to Vietnam. I truly did not want to go, but I had no other choice.

Back in Da Nang, I met up with the Team where we all

swapped stories about our break. I told the team about my time with Rachel Sanders and made a point of telling Gunner, Duffield and Combs that she was white and that I stayed at her house. I went into detail about her mother and father making me dinner every night. But most of all, I told them about how I made love to this Australian white girl and how she liked it.

Man, the looks on their faces were priceless. If Gunner had been armed, I believe he would have shot me on the spot.

CHAPTER 33

FIRST LOSS

We got our next mission. There was a report of a downed pilot from an F-105 Thunderchief, an Air Force fighter-bomber. We were charged with recovering the pilot and destroying the aircraft.

The team left at 1300 hours. The weather was very bad, a monsoon rain that came down in sheets. The wind had the rain hitting us at a sideways angle. We could hardly see three feet in front of ourselves.

Our drop-off was north of Hue, in a dense jungle full of very large jackfruit trees. If you've never heard of jackfruit, it's the largest tree-borne fruit, about 2 feet long and capable of growing up to 120 pounds each. Each tree can have 15 or 20 of the fruits.

Then there were the banyan trees, with very large roots that circle the trunk from the top of the tree down to the ground. The roots intertwined around the base of the tree could be 70 feet around.

Hidden in the trees were vipers. We called them three steps, because if you were bitten that's all you would get: three steps. So we had to have eyes looking up, down, behind us, on the sides. Our heads were continuously on a swivel.

Gunner was taking point. He came across some punji stake traps, pointed sticks are stuck in a hole (pointed ends up, of course) and covered with brush for an unsuspecting soldier to step into. Gunner was able to guide us around them expertly. We did not trip any of the traps, as that would have given our presence away.

Using the trees and heavy foliage for cover, we moved slowly through the jungle. We located the pilot, unharmed, in an abandoned Buddhist temple. He advised us that there had been heavy NVA patrols out looking for him.

We started out for the downed airplane after dark. This time Gardner took point. We were moving at a good clip, far too fast for my liking. I thought it would be too easy to miss something. It became even harder to remain fully aware of our surroundings as it got darker.

I was just six steps behind Gardner on point when he tripped a booby trap. I heard the sound of a heavy snap: tree branches breaking and vines tearing. A huge section of a log came swinging down. It had sharp pieces of metal embedded in it.

"Look out!" I yelled to Gardner, but I was too late. The log and its metallic inserts took Gardner's head off cleanly at the shoulders. I froze in place and fell to my knees. There was a lump in my throat and my heart sank. I knew immediately that I had just lost my good friend and Frog Buddy.

The team and the pilot took care of Gardner's remains. No man left behind. They put his body over my shoulder and his head in Combs' backpack.

The trip back to the swift boat was quiet the entire time, none of the usual chatter or banter back and forth.

Gardner, Ortega and I were what we called Cut Buddies to the Bone. That means when one gets cut the others bleed. I never had a brother like those two, and now our little brotherhood was down one.

The pilot we had rescued gave his condolences and thanked us for saving him. Had he been captured he would have been headed for the Hanoi Hilton on the other side of the DMZ.

Once back in Da Nang, we had our mission debrief and went over the facts that led to the death of one of the Team. Now that we were down a man, we knew things would be harder until we got a replacement.

That night I was hard pressed to get some rest. I could not get Gardner out of my mind. The scene would repeatedly play in slow motion all night long. I could see the trap spring and see it coming down. I could hear myself yelling, "Gardner get down!"

I asked if I could pack up Gardner's gear locker. It was one of the hardest things I ever had to do. I gave his possessions to the commanding officer to be sent back home. Then I asked, "What about his surfboard?" I found it hard to even say his name, Frances Gardner.

After a few days had passed, Gardner was all boxed up with the Red White and Blue covering his casket. He was loaded on a C130 with a lot of other dead soldiers, along with some wounded soldiers headed stateside.

Gunner, Duffield and Combs had nothing to say other than "One down and two to go," meaning me and Ortega.

After seeing our brother off for the last time Ortega and I went into town for a drink. We got to the Non-Commissioned Officer's club and raised a few beers to our fallen brother. A SEAL till the end.

Republic of Vietnam
Cross for Gallantry
With Plum

CHAPTER 34
A MAN DOWN

It was hard coming to grips with the loss of my brother and friend, Gardner. I could not wrap my head around it. I kept going over what happened in my mind, over and over and over again, wondering if there was something I could have done differently that would have saved his life.

Ortega could see that my mind was a million miles off. "Watts, it's not your fault," he said. "The team has been running on luck over one and a half years. We all knew someone's number was going to get punched; it was just a matter of when."

I felt even more hatred for the enemy forces. I started praying more often, and harder, for God to take this hatred I was feeling from my heart. But the more I prayed the more I would wonder if God really existed. Why would God not take one of the enemy? Why one of the good guys? I had been taught that faith is the belief in what cannot be seen, and hope in what is yet to come. But I was losing my faith and trust in God, and more and more I felt I had to rely on my own wiles and have faith only in myself to get home.

I wanted to reach out to Gardner's father to send my condolences and to see how he was doing. The man was in a dark place. Gardner was his only child. Gardner had told his father about our team, mostly about me and Ortega. I had to be careful about what I wrote to him, as most of the things we were doing in Vietnam were confidential. I kept my letter soft and easygoing. In Mr. Gardner's response, Ortega and I were given an open invitation to visit him when we made it back home.

The Team was coming close to the end of its tour in-country. Command asked if we would stay on for another full tour, which would be a year; if not, would we consider at least six months. We were offered a $1,000 bonus for another tour.

Command gave us time to think it over. I was not sure if I could do this again. I was not as gung ho for another tour as I had been the first time I re-upped, almost two years prior. And I did not like how I was becoming emotionally entrenched in this place. I was not in a good way mentally.

Plus there was another war raging at home, a war of racial freedom and independence for millions of black and brown people. I worried about what was happening back in America.

While we thought it over, it was time to get back to work hunting and killing the enemy. In my present state of mind there was nothing I wanted to do more than kill me some Viet Cong. Once I had chastised Gunner for dehumanizing the inhabitants of Vietnam, but now I was just as guilty of doing so to the enemy.

Command was in bad need of intelligence, not just from our eyes but firsthand from the enemy. We were tasked with capturing more NVA soldiers. It made me think of an old Western TV show, *Wanted Dead or Alive* with Steve McQueen, and I was thinking I preferred the enemy more dead than alive. Hunting the Viet Cong was satisfying in that I felt I could get some justice for Gardner. I thought he would like that.

The team would be out for two weeks at a time. If we ran across low level Viet Cong we would initiate a firefight, killing as many as we could and doing so as often as we could. We would bring back officers and any documents we could find.

I was getting good at hunting, and even better at killing. Combs was exceptionally good at tracking. He would often talk about years of hunting deer and bear in the mountains of Tennessee and these skills proved to be a major asset to the team.

The intelligence that we had gathered started paying off. Command learned that the NVA was moving troops and heavy ordinance across the Demilitarized Zone. American B-52s began carpet bombing these North Vietnamese forces in the DMZ. Command wanted eyes on the targets to help determine the results of the bombing raids. SEAL Team One was ordered north, along with several other black ops teams, to scout out the targets.

After kitting up, our Team took a chopper north to our target drop zone. The chopper hovered in position while the Team fast-roped down to the Landing Zone. We were tasked with searching 24 square kilometers, a little over 15 miles. While on patrol we logged a large, targeted bomb site that showed a great amount of destroyed ordinance, mostly Chinese artillery in origin.

On day six we ran across a joint NVA and Viet Cong patrol and a firefight ensued. We all took cover. Gunner, Combs and Duffield went left, and the Lieutenant, Ortega and I took right.

Duffield let loose with his M79 and bodies went flying. In return, rapid fire machine gun rounds whizzed past my face so closely that I could feel the heat.

Ortega yelled to Gunner, "RPG!" An enemy soldier had fired a rocket-propelled grenade, a shoulder-fired rocket launcher with an explosive warhead. Gunner had been taking cover behind a very large jackfruit tree when the explosive shell detonated near him.

Gunner took some shrapnel in his lower right shoulder.

He was bleeding badly. Combs packed the wound and gave Gunner some morphine for the pain.

Ortega and I moved to the enemy's right flank and tossed in some Willie Peter (white phosphorus bombs). The NVA and Viet Cong soldiers started screaming and yelling, rolling on the ground to try to stop the burning. They had no such luck.

We had to get Gunner out of there, but our planned extraction point had been a clearing about two kilometers away and the entire area was swarming with the enemy. The going would be too slow with Gunner so badly wounded.

The jungle was too dense for a chopper to land and take us out so we had to find another clearing where we could get picked up. Someone spotted a cave on the side of a mountain and we took cover there while we worked on stabilizing Gunner. He was losing a lot of blood and needed a battlefield blood transfusion if he was going to make it.

Gunner and I had the same blood type, no one else on the Team, so it would be up to me to save the racist asshole's life. I asked myself, Why in hell would I want to help him after all the shit he put me through? The world would be better off without him in it.

But who was I to judge? I decided. So I went through with it.

Command contacted the Lieutenant and gave him new coordinates for a chopper pickup. We made it out of there without any further injuries.

Blood Brothers

As soon as we got back to Da Nang, Gunner was taken to the base hospital. He had the golden ticket home: an injury serious enough to prevent him from performing further service, but not fatal or too serious like the loss of a limb.

After a week had passed the Team went to the hospital to

see Gunner. As we entered his room I was holding a boom box that was blasting a James Brown song: "Say It Loud, I'm Black and I'm Proud." It was a far cry from the country music that Gunner listened to.

I went over to his bed with the boom box and Gunner shouted over the noise, "What the hell is this coon music you're playing?"

I replied, "Do you remember telling me that even just 1% Nigger blood makes you a Nigger? Do you remember telling me that? Well, welcome to Soul Town, Gunner. Didn't anyone tell you where your blood transfusion came from? You are now officially a Nigger because you got my Nigger blood. And when your firstborn son comes out looking like me it'll be because he has my Nigger blood too."

You could see the anger and hatred welling in his eyes. Before he could gather himself to reply I turned and walked out of the room, a huge smile on my face and a jump in my step.

Making Peace

Before Gunner was shipped home, he told Combs to ask me to come see him. Against my better judgment I went to visit him.

I stood in the doorway to his hospital room and said, "You wanted to see me?"

He motioned for me to come in with his good arm, and then he extended his hand for me to shake it. I ignored it.

"Duffield told me what you did," he began. "You gave me your blood and saved my life."

I waited silently for him to continue, my arms folded across my chest. His hand was still being offered to me.

He went on in a serious tone. "I apologize from the bottom of my heart. Over the last two years I have treated you with total disrespect, and by doing so I dishonored myself and the

Team. If you choose not to shake my hand or forgive me I will understand. But I hope that you can find it in your heart to forgive me."

I paused a moment to think it over, then I came forward and clasped his hand in mine. "I forgive you, brother," I said. And for the first time ever I felt like I was talking to him as a brother SEAL.

CHAPTER 35
END OF TOUR

Meanwhile I still had to decide whether I wanted to serve another tour.

Why was I here in Vietnam? I asked myself. To play God? To take life, and in Gunner's case even to give life? No, this was not what I had signed up for. I was there fighting for a people I did not know and had even learned to hate. I couldn't do this anymore. I was not signing on for another tour. It was time to go home.

But I still had a tour to finish. With Gunner heading back to the good old U. S. of A. we were down two guys now, so we were looking to get some new blood on the Team.

Our platoon strength was too short to take on a full mission, so we were told to stand down until replacements could be acquired. We were out of action for almost two weeks.

During that off time I worked out with my taekwondo instructor, Master Hoon. It was good having something else to focus on.

But all good things come to an end and our break was over. We were assigned a mission.

Before the mission briefing, I was told I could sit this one out because my time in-country and my enlistment was almost over. But I figured my platoon needed me, so instead of standing down I agreed to this one last mission.

At least it wasn't our typical hunt and kill assignment. The objective was to escort a group of medical non-combatants who were vaccinating and treating villagers to a safe zone in Hue. A chopper flew us into our target zone, a village that had about 15 huts built on stilts about 6 feet off the ground. The huts were made of sticks and had palm thatched roofs.

We searched the entire village for the medical team but found no one there. In some of the huts we found the dismembered arms of children who had been vaccinated. The Viet Cong cut off those arms in which the vaccine had been injected.

After searching the surrounding area, we came across a cave. The aid workers, as well as some villagers, were hiding inside. We learned that the women in the village had been raped and brutalized and the men conscripted or killed.

The medical team was comprised of four men and two women. Fear was written all over their faces. We announced ourselves as U.S. Navy SEALs, there to take them to Hue. The medical team jumped up and ran over to us, thanking us with big hugs. They asked if we could also take the women and children from the village. We did not have room for the villagers on the return chopper.

There were no healthy males in the cave, just old men and children. Many of them had tourniquets from where the Viet Cong had amputated their arms. The Viet Cong had conscripted the other men and boys to fight for them. Sadly, we had to leave the rest of the villagers behind.

We got the medical team back to Hue with no contact with the Viet Cong, although some of us were angry enough that we had wanted to come across a few enemy soldiers.

Let Bygones Be Bygones
Afterwards, Duffield and Combs came up to me together. Combs told me, "Everything we ever heard about Black

soldiers not facing the enemy or having our backs was just another lie. One we had been taught to believe. You showed us the right way, Watts. We wanted to say that we're really sorry."

Duffield said, "We may never be friends but maybe we can finally be SEAL brothers."

I accepted their apology and shook each man's hand in turn.

My enlistment was almost over, and in February 1969 I would be out. I was what was called a short timer, meaning I had less than 90 days left in-country. I had a short timer's calendar, a picture of a naked woman divided into 90 days. I would color in each day until I reached home. Use your imagination as to where home was.

As time grew shorter our missions grew fewer. I asked Ortega if he was going do another tour.

"No way, man. I'm going home to Texas. Why would I stay here another year? Why, are you staying?"

"Nah, I already turned down the thousand dollar bonus to stay another year. I'm going home to Philadelphia. Anyway, there's a whole different war to fight back home for us Black people."

There was no reason for me to stay, I had accomplished all I set out to do. I had no clue how I was going to be able to help out back home, but I had to try.

Home. Man, did that sound good. But as good as it sounded, it had an air of uncertainty. I had learned to SCUBA dive, jump from a plane, and kill people in various ways. How could I turn those skills into a job back in the states? I was also told that Vietnam vets were not very popular at home, especially Black vets.

Vietnam Service

Vietnam Campaign

CHAPTER 36

HISTORY LESSON

The SEALs were some of the most highly decorated units in Vietnam. They accounted for almost half of all POWs rescued. By the end of 1970 they had killed over 2,000 Viet Cong and captured about 2,700, many of whom were important members of the enemy military. On the other hand, over nine years in Vietnam, only 36 or so SEALs were killed.

CHAPTER 37

BACK TO AMERICA

I was now 21, and in mid-February Ortega and I went out for one last drink. One drink turned into a great number of drinks. I got so drunk that I don't remember everything that happened that night.

I vaguely remember the next day, my final day. Ortega put me on a Tiger jetliner, the charter service the government used to fly vets stateside with a stopover in Seoul, South Korea. When we landed in San Diego, I got off the plane and was handed my discharge papers and a one-way ticket to Philadelphia. This was all done on the tarmac.

A Hero's Greeting

All of us vets were advised not to wear our uniforms due to the protests against the war. As we exited the airport there was a large crowd of people protesting the war, mostly college age by the look of them. They were spitting at us, throwing rotten fruit and vegetables, and calling us baby killers and all of kinds of foul names. It took all of my self control not to knock the shit out of some of them. I thought to myself, They don't know me or the things I have seen. They don't know what I had to do to fight for this country. A country that rejects me because I'm Black.

I walked away, out of the Navy and out of the SEALs. It was very scary not knowing what tomorrow would bring. I had no job, just my muster out pay of $500.

Layover in Los Angeles

I took a Greyhound bus to Los Angeles and stayed there for a couple of weeks. I wanted to get my bearings until I felt like I was home, until I felt like I was myself again, before I went back to my family.

I met a young lady who happened to be a dancer on a new television program, a TV show with dancers and star performers called *Soul Train*.

"I could get you on the show," she offered.

"Ah, I don't know how to dance," I told her.

"I could teach you."

"That would be nice, but I have to be up front with you. I'm staying in a cheap hotel because I have just gotten back from Vietnam. I've only been back stateside for two weeks now."

I was afraid that the truth would turn her off. Instead, she asked me to stay with her at her apartment! Of course, I jumped at the offer.

I finally called my mom a couple weeks later. She was glad to hear from me but wanted to know how I could be calling from Vietnam.

"I … I've been home for almost a month," I told her.

"Where are you?" she asked.

"Los Angeles."

"Los Angeles?" Man, did she get angry. She said, "If you don't bring your Black ass home I'm coming out there to get you."

I left Los Angeles without saying a word to my lady friend, on the next plane east to Philadelphia.

CHAPTER 38
HOME AGAIN

After landing in Philadelphia, I took a taxi home. The car pulled up and I got out, a big smile on my face as I looked at a very large banner that had been hung across the front of the house that said "Welcome home John."

The house was full with all my brothers and sisters, except for my brother Jeff, who was now in Vietnam himself. All of my childhood friends, people I had not seen in almost two years, were there. Mom made all my favorite foods: potato salad, fried chicken, collard greens and red velvet cakes.

I should have been having the time of my life. But being home was very unsettling. I did not know how to talk to all of these people, or what to talk about. Everyone keep asking me the same thing: "How was it over there?" and "Did you kill some of them?" I thought to myself, What kind of fucking question is that?

Mom stood up for me. She told everyone, "Leave John alone. He just got home and I'm sure that is not what he wants to talk about now."

The party went on until the wee hours of the morning. I was eventually able to relax and feel like myself.

Panther Power

While I was back in the States I heard about a group called

the Black Panthers. This was a group of Black freedom fighters who were especially big in California. Their founder was Huey P. Newton and the membership of this growing group fighting for social justice included Angela Davis, H. Rap Brown, and Bobby Seals.

I did not know much about the Black Panthers or their political agenda but what I did know about was their outreach to the community; like feeding kids breakfast and tutoring the same kids in the afternoon. Philadelphia had its own chapter, relatively small (about 180 members). There were offices in Germantown, South Philadelphia, and North Philadelphia. The Philadelphia chapter followed the lead of the headquarters in California.

Philadelphia Police Commissioner Frank Rizzo had a hard-on for harassing the Panthers. He coordinated raids of the Panther headquarters in North Philadelphia and Germantown. The raids were to take place at 8:00 a.m. on a Monday morning, when the kids were being fed breakfast. The Panthers were made to strip almost naked, and paraded outside to embarrass and make a spectacle of them. The newspapers were there taking pictures.

I had given thought to joining the Panthers but decided against it. I'd had enough of fighting and just wanted some peace.

CHAPTER 39
BACK TO WORK

I was home for three days before a cousin found me a job at a Philadelphia hospital working in the central sterile supply department. The job was easy, all I had to do was put things in an autoclave for a few hours until they were sterile.

I was still not quite myself. I seemed to be always on hyper alert. One day my female boss came up behind me and accidentally spooked me. Without thinking I punched her in the face. She didn't turn me in, though; I got lucky.

I only worked there for a month, however. A doctor called for a Striker bed frame for a patient. I delivered it to him and, as I had been instructed, began to tell the doctor about a new locking mechanism on the bed. He did not want to hear what I was trying to tell him, so when he put the patient in the bed and turned it over the patient fell out and hit the floor. Then the doctor called me a dumb Nigger. Next thing I knew, he was on the floor next to the patient, and I was out of a job.

I found a part-time job teaching karate downtown. My class was composed of nursing students and people from the neighborhood. One of them was a full blooded Chippewa from Canada by the name of Krystal Wilhelmsen. Krystal was very fair with dark black hair. If you did not know better you would think she was white.

We hit it off just great and started dating. Krystal lived in a nursing dorm at 8th and Vine. Students had a very strict curfew, and she had to be in the dorm by 11 p.m. every night. One night my brother Jeff and I took Krystal home and left her at her dorm.

A man who lived across the street stood in his doorway and started yelling at me for no reason. "I see you, you filthy Nigger. I see you coming and going with that white girl." The man pulled a .45 caliber automatic from behind his body and shouted, "If I see you around her again, I'll kill you."

My anger overcame my senses and I yelled back, "Who the fuck do you think you are?"

Jeff was pulling on my arm, saying, "Come on, John, come on." But I was angry beyond description. My stomach was tied in knots and I could not walk away.

I walked up the steps to the man's front door, clearly surprising the man because he didn't shoot me. I grabbed his wrist with my left hand, and jammed the slide of his .45 with my right. I pulled the pistol from his hand and, having remembered my years of practice with firearms, disassembled it before the man's very eyes. It turned out that there were no bullets in the gun. I finished breaking the gun down and handed it back to the man in pieces.

Several weeks later Krystal and I were walking along 7th street when, all of a sudden, a white man came running out of a dry cleaners. Behind him an elderly Asian woman was running and yelling. "Stop that man! He just robbed and beat me!"

Like a fool I took off running after the man. I chased him for two blocks before the police rolled in front of me in a police transport truck called a paddy wagon. They cut me off from the robber, jumped out of the paddy wagon, and grabbed me. They accused me of the robbery and assault, cuffed me, and threw me in the back of the transport. After being bounced off the walls of the wagon a few times I was taken to the police station at 9th and South Street.

It took several hours before the old lady came in and told

the police they had arrested the wrong person, and that the guy who had robbed her had been a white man. This was clearly a case of being arrested for running while black.

Odd Jobs

I did not have much in the way of work skills, having been in the Navy from the time I was 17 until I was 21. And with people's distaste for the war, finding a good paying job was hard.

Over the course of several years, I worked for different finance companies as a bill collector and repo man. My next job was with a business called Town Finance at 8th and Market. They were a company that made secured loans and were looking for someone to be a debt collector and do repossession work in North Philadelphia. The white guys in the office did not like the idea of going into Black and Latino neighborhoods to collect money. What they did not understand is how most people paid their bills: if you owed a debt you expected the debt collector to eventually show up in person and you would then give them money, no problem. The bread man and milk man show up, and you pay them. The same line of thinking holds for loan companies, too: people didn't have a problem paying their debts, they just waited until someone knocked on their door.

I once worked for a business called Rent-A-Center. They rented appliances and televisions to poor people. When the customers stopped paying or were unable to pay, I was sent out to repossess what had been rented. The company gave me paperwork authorizing me to enter a customer's house after notifying the police of my purpose. There were times I would take a 25-inch TV and throw it down the steps or out a window, then rush to get out of there before things turned violent.

Eventually I quit and found a new job with Terminix Pest Control. I dealt with termites and rodents. It was all work on commission, and I made good money.

The pest control business was very competitive. Another business by the name of Dynamite Pest Control had placed an ad in the paper for a pest control manager, as the business was looking to expand its client base beyond the streets of North Philadelphia, West Philadelphia, and South Philadelphia. I went for an interview, and the manager liked the way I spoke. He told me I sounded white, and white people would feel comfortable talking to me. He offered me $500 a week to manage his business. That was more than I had ever made doing collections.

I increased his business by 75% and the money was very good. Unfortunately, I later found out that Dynamite Pest Control was laundering money and hiding drugs for a drug dealer by the name of Big George. That was when I quit; I wanted no part of anything to do with drugs.

My next job was the West Philadelphia Boys and Girls Club at 35th and Haverford. I was a counselor for young boys. All the kids were from the rough side of West Philadelphia. Most of them were from single family homes with no male figure in the house.

They had never been outside the city, so I took them on camping trips. Many of them did not know how to swim, so I gave them swimming lessons. Some of them needed to learn how to protect themselves, so those I taught karate.

I would also help the kids when they would go to juvenile court, by talking with the judges and explaining their circumstances.

CHAPTER 40
LOVE LIFE

In March of 1973 I was 25. I had it in my head that I should start thinking about getting married. I asked my cousin Jaletha to introduce me to one of her girlfriends who was also looking to get married. "Ja", as we called her, was reluctant because all her girlfriends were older than me. But she eventually gave in.

A few weeks later, on March 23, Ja brought a blind date to meet me at the Boys and Girls Club. Ja introduced me to Patricia Ford. She wore a pair of hip hugger bell bottom jeans with a chain belt, a white midriff blouse, and sandals. Her hair was styled after the Black freedom fighter Angela Davis, in a big afro, and she wore large hoop earrings. She was beautiful.

We both felt like we had met each other before. After talking we realized we had gone on a blind date in April of 1968. She was the one who had thought I had too much of the war in me.

The next day, March 24th, was a Saturday. Patricia and I, along with Ja and six other cousins, drove to New York to visit my grandmother for her birthday. That night, all of us went to a club in Greenwich Village called The Raspberry Freeze. We had a great time. We all slept at my grandmother's house, then went home the next day.

I was in more of a hurry to get married than Patricia was, as after eight years of marriage she had been divorced for about a year. She did not know if she wanted to get married again so soon. But two weeks later I asked Patricia to marry me, and she said yes. We were married four months after. The courtship went by very fast but we had a great time and I was sooo looking forward to making Patricia my wife.

Patricia owned a house in Germantown, a part of Philadelphia. We lived there after we got married, along with her two children, Sheralyn Fortune and John Fortune. Life had turned out pretty good for me.

John and Patricia Watts

CHAPTER 41
IN A BAD PLACE

My nightmares were beginning to take over. Violent dreams were invading my bedroom, with my fists punching the bed and feet kicking the air at whatever was threatening me in my subconscious. Many a time my wife would wake me because I was thrashing and yelling in my sleep. One dream in particular had me reliving the loss of my friend Gardner. It would play over and over many nights, like a broken record. I talked to a Veterans Administration psychiatrist who had me try something called immersive therapy. He had me pick out one traumatic event and repeat it over and over and over. The idea was that by doing this, it would take up less space in my unconscious mind. Instead, it only made me more and more angry.

I was having survivor's guilt. I had been just a few feet behind Gardner when the trap that took his life was sprung, and the fact that he had been taking my turn on point only made it worse. Thoughts of taking my life started creeping into my mind, and it was becoming harder to deal with the memories on a day to day basis.

I broke down and told my VA psychiatrist what was going on in my head. The doctor immediately had me admitted to the Coatesville VA hospital. I was in the psychiatric ward for two months. During that period of time I learned how to perform meditation and mindfulness breathing. I attended one on one therapy as well as group therapy.

When I came home I no longer had any thoughts of harming myself, but the anger was still there.

John and Patricia Watts

CHAPTER 42
SURPRISE
REUNION

One day I got a call from my mother, who told me there was someone at her house to see me, a guy I had been in Vietnam with. He said his name was Charles Hazen. I had no idea who that was.

Mom put him on the phone. It turned out to be Gunner. All that time I had never known his true name.

I thought to myself, What is he doing here? As we talked he told me he was with his wife, and he wanted her to meet the man who had saved his life. He was in Philadelphia on his way to Florida. I invited him to have dinner with Patricia and me.

The doorbell rang and when I answered it, there was Gunner and his wife, Marcia. He introduced Marcia to Patricia and me, then stepped in and gave me a great big hug. That was very unexpected.

I asked Gunner what he was doing this far north. He said he had met his wife in Ohio, married her, and they were now on their way to Florida. He was taking a job as a sheriff there.

I took Gunner aside so Patricia could talk with Marcia. I asked him, "Did you ever tell your wife about what we had done during the war?"

He shook his head. "No way. All of our missions are still classified, as well as us even being SEALs. I told Marcia that we were part of a river team working the Perfume River. She never asked me for any stories. She knows people don't like to talk about their experiences over there."

The dinner table had been set with our best china, flatware and crystal glasses. I wanted Gunner to see we were not heathens. We had roast beef, mashed potatoes, gravy and green peas. We talked about our lives after Vietnam.

At one point during dinner Gunner started talking about the time he was wounded and the blood transfusion I gave him to save his life. Much to my surprise, Gunner also told them about how he had called me Shadow and what the intent was behind the nickname. A stillness settled over the table, and Patricia looked at me as if to say, Why was he in our house and at our table?

I smiled as I looked at Patricia, then at Marcia, then at Gunner. I whispered, "He asked for my forgiveness, and as a follower of Jesus Christ, I gave it to him."

After dinner we sat and talked for a while longer, then Gunner and his wife had to leave on the next leg of their journey to Florida. It had been very good seeing Gunner and meeting his wife. I did not think we would ever be close friends or see each other again, but I was able to say goodbye to a SEAL brother.

CHAPTER 43
MORE TROUBLES

A few years later, in 1976, our first child together was born. We named her Zakia Patricia Watts and she made me the happiest man in the world.

When Zakia was four we took her to see Santa Claus at a local mall. The line was long, and everyone was being patient. As we stood in line, Patricia was behind me, and I heard her having words with a man behind her. I turned and asked, "What's the problem?"

Patricia replied, "This man told his wife that if these Niggers weren't in line, they could be next." She looked at the man, some nothing slob in my opinion, and told him, "Is the pot calling the kettle black?"

The woman told her husband, "Don't mess with them." She was smart. Her husband was not, as I was already seeing red from his behavior and the smug look on his face.

Next thing I knew I had launched a back kick to the man's chest, and he went flying across the floor. Patricia grabbed me by the arm and took me out of the mall before any police came. This was my first time showing signs of PTSD.

Job Offer
In 1979 my SEAL brother Ortega gave me a call, saying things were hard going for Vietnam vets in Texas (especially

for Mexicans). He said finding a good job was almost impossible. He was working as a day laborer in the fields picking vegetables and fruit. He hated it, and felt like he was being treated like less than a man.

Ortega told me he had found an advertisement in *Soldier of Fortune* magazine seeking vets with jungle experience to help train a group in Nicaragua called Contras. He wanted to know if I was interested.

I asked him. "Didn't you get enough fighting in 'Nam?"

"Yeah, but I felt like a man there. Here I don't. And this way I can support my family."

The next call I got about Ortega was a year later, from his wife. Ortega had been killed and his body was being shipped home.

Growing My Job Skills

I was still working at the Boys and Girls Club. I had single mothers calling me to help their sons who were going to court or having trouble at school. Patricia and I were still newly married, and she did not like single women calling me for help when I was supposed to be "off duty." I had to quit.

I found an ad in the local paper for collectors at a bank, Advanta National. But the main requirement was computer skills, and I had none. My neighbor and friend, Terry, was a computer technical support person for a big company in the city. He offered to teach me. Terry gave me enough of a basic understanding for me to apply and get the job.

Advanta National was a credit card bank that issued Master Card and Visa. After I worked there for two years in collections, a spot in the credit card fraud department opened up. I applied and got the new position.

As the years passed my skill at investigating credit card fraud got better and better. I specialized in Nigerian fraud rings, triads, tongs, and Black Dragon Vietnamese fraud groups. These were cases that got reported to the United States Secret Service. When the Secret Service picked up a case for prosecution, the case manager would be subpoenaed for court. I was subpoenaed on numerous occasions and represented the bank in courts all over the country: in Las Vegas, San Diego, New York, Philadelphia, Boston and Phoenix. The bank's success rate in recovering stolen funds and merchandise that had been bought with credit cards caught the attention of other banks. I then became a part of a small team that would help train other banks on the investigation techniques we used to recover funds and merchandise.

After 12 years working for Advanta, it was sold and became Colonial National Bank. The new bank started laying off personnel and closed the office where I had been working. I found a job with GMAC Mortgage, back in collections. I worked in the collections department for a year and a half, then used the skills I had obtained as a credit card fraud investigator to segue into mortgage fraud.

This type of fraud was very different; it involved realtors, appraisers and sellers. I enjoyed this type of investigative work, finding it to be challenging and mentally stimulating. Finding the fraudsters and making them pay the company back was a huge reward.

One of my last cases was for a law firm in Philadelphia by the name of Wilkes & McHugh. They offered me a job investigating geriatric abuse and I accepted. My position involved locating witnesses to abuse that took place at nursing homes all over the state. My pay was $800 a week plus expenses. Thanks to overtime, my paycheck would sometimes be $1,500 a week.

The Anger Never Goes Away

As time went on, I found myself getting into more and more fights. One Saturday afternoon in the 1990s I was working on our house and needed some supplies. I hopped into my car and headed to a supply store. As I approached a stop sign there was a man with his family leaving the VFW across the street. We both pulled out into traffic at the same time and almost collided. The man rolled down his window and yelled, "Nigger, you can't drive! I should beat your black ass like Rodney King."

I got out of my car and approached him. As I stood in front of his car I took off my steel toed work boots, because I fully intended to kick his ass but I did not want to kill the man. He started his car and tried to run me over. Without thinking I jumped onto the hood of the car, and grabbed onto the open moon roof.

The man sped off, me still holding onto the roof. I pulled myself up with one hand, reached down through the moon roof, and pounded the driver's head with my other hand. The man was flying down the street with me still holding on.

He drove straight to the Abington Police station. I calmly got down from the car and, in my stocking feet, strolled into the police station lobby and took a seat. The man's family entered and sat down as well, but the driver himself was pacing up and down and spitting venom at me. "Okay, Nigger, you done it now. You are going to jail, you motherfucking bastard."

He called me a Nigger several more times, each time putting his face right in front of mine. But I knew the police station was heavily monitored with video and audio surveillance, so I just sat there not saying a word. I let him do all the talking and yelling.

What he did not know was that I was a member of the Abington Civilian Police Academy. The Academy was a group of civilians who were taught police procedure and, if needed, helped the police in times of emergency.

Police officers interviewed us in separate rooms. One of the policemen knew me and came into my room. He asked,

"John, what's going on? Who is this guy? We saw the tape from his ranting in the lobby. Do you know him?"

"Never met him before today. But let me tell you what happened."

After I finished the policeman told me to call my wife to come and get me. I was allowed to leave. The driver, a man from Philadelphia, was charged with ethnic intimidation.

Traveling down under

CHAPTER 44
GLOBE TROTTING

It was 1980 when my wife and I took our first big trip out of the country. It was the first of what would become many international vacations.

South America

We found a tour of the Amazon that included time in Lima, Peru. I was really looking forward to seeing the Amazon Jungle. After arriving in Peru and getting settled, we started to explore. We learned so much about the Incan civilization and their fall after the Spanish invaded that part of the world. Francisco Pizarro invaded Peru in 1532, and 168 Spanish soldiers captured Emperor Huayna Capac. The Incas fled to a mountain fortress 14,000 feet high in the Peruvian Andes. Machu Picchu is the name of the city.

Our next stop was the Amazon Jungle. We flew from Lima to Aketos, a small town on the mouth of the Amazon River. Then we took a boat upriver, where we stopped and spent time with the Yangel tribe. As we kicked through the jungle to the Yangel village, I loved being surrounded by the jungle's lush green plants and trees, the chatter of the monkeys and the sound of the birds. The trees were massive, with very large roots at their bases. The roots alone were taller than me, and the trees were 40 to 50 feet high. Their leaves formed canopies that blotted out the sun.

When we arrived at the village there were about 6 or 7 grass huts. The people were short, and the woman were bare breasted with grass skirts. The children wore no clothes and the men wore a material made from pounded tree bark. We were told at the beginning of our trip that the natives had no need for money so we should bring things to trade. We brought fishing line, disposable rain gear, cloth from my wife's sewing with large flowers printed on it, and lollipops and candy for the kids. Patricia was trading her cloth with the women for some handcrafted items but when the men saw how colorful it was they pushed the women out the way and took over the bargaining process.

The Akuntsu people were headhunters about 30 years ago and they would shrink heads to about the size of a softball. I wanted to trade for a shrunken head but my wife Patricia said, "No way, buddy, you are not bringing that thing into my house."

We had dinner with the Akuntsu over a very large fire pit. We were served stuffed tapioca root and chewawa, a white meat fish weighing in at about 80 lbs that was grilled over an open flame. After dinner Patricia and I went with our guide for a canoe ride on the river.

At night the sky was like nothing my wife had ever seen. But to me it was just like the sky in Vietnam, trillions of stars in a blanket of blackness. I dove from the canoe into the Amazon River, not thinking about the many things that could go wrong (like cayman, anaconda, and that very, very small fish that swims up the head of a man's penis to lay its eggs).

Back to Vietnam

God has blessed my wife and I to have been able to have traveled so extensively. We have traveled from the roof of the world in Kathmandu, to the Pyramids in Egypt, to the Great Wall of China, and to the Great Barrier Reef in Australia. But it was years before I decided to go back to

Vietnam.

Before booking the trip I talked to several Vietnam veterans who had taken similar trips to Vietnam. They all recommended going back. It had helped them reset their minds and assisted in dealing with their PTSD.

I knew this trip to Vietnam was going to be hard for me, but it was something I needed for closure. It was hard preparing myself to go back to the place that haunted my dreams, where I knew I would relive the loss of so many friends and fellow American soldiers.

The trip was to be three weeks, starting in Saigon (which is now Ho Chi Minh City). After getting through immigration and out into the city, the smell of Vietnam hit me and memories came back in my mind in a flash. Where we refer to it as the Vietnam War, the Vietnamese people call it the American War. That alone showed there was a different mindset for the people there, as they had become indoctrinated by a communist government. During my time in Vietnam during the war I had never gotten to Saigon, but the smell of the city reminded me of how Da nang had been way back when. But instead of hundreds of bicycles and rickshaws in the street there were hundreds of motor bikes and scooters.

Part of our trip included viewing the Chi-Chi Tunnels. These were where the Viet Cong stored food, ammunition, and weapons and hid out from the Americans. During the war the tunnels were loaded with traps. American soldiers who ventured into the tunnels were called Tunnel Rats. Many of them were killed or severely wounded. When we got there I could not do it. I could not make myself go into those tunnels.

We took a short cruise down the Mekong River, where there were floating markets with fresh vegetables and fish. You could also stop at restaurants for a meal. We had jackfruit and lionfish. The fish is the size of a dinner plate and the dorsal fin and tail fin are heavily boned, so the fish was served upright like it was swimming.

Out next stop was the city of Da nang. A new high rise skyline gave the city a different appearance, but when I looked closer at the back streets and alleys there it was, the Da nang I remembered. Small shops and food stands sold much of the same foods I ate before: grilled monkey meat on a stick, pork and fish.

I took a side trip to China Beach, where the Team would go for beach parties and swimming and my buddy Gardner used his surfboard. The waves were very good, and Gardner would go surfing when we had some down time.

From Da nang we were off to Hue, the old imperial city. After getting there I asked our guide to take me to the Nguyen Hoang steel bridge over the Perfume River. It had been rebuilt along with the boat dock where a mortar had taken out our PBR and crew.

It was a short walk to the Citadel, where our team had taken cover from the Viet Cong and the NVA. Standing on the outside, looking up at the high walls, I remembered taking heavy small arms and automatic weapons fire.

I walked through the gate where the walls were pockmarked from bullets, and memories of the war came flooding in. I looked at a lion dog set in front of a temple and remembered when I had taken cover behind it. I could see myself as if from outside of my own body. The bullet marks were still there.

The next stop was Hanoi, the seat of Ho Chi Minh's communist government. The people in Vietnam refer to Ho Chi Minh as Papa Ho.

While we were in-country the Team never went above the area demarcated as the Demilitarized Zone as it was supposed to be no-man's-land. Part of the tour included the infamous P.O.W. camp known as the Hanoi Hilton. Propaganda photos that lined the walls showed Americans having turkey dinner for Thanksgiving and playing basketball in a yard. It also made the living quarters look to be clean and accommodating.

Patricia and I took a night off from the guided tour and went to dinner in town. We found the restaurant that Anthony Bourdain took then-President Barack Obama to for dinner. The restaurant was not big or fancy, it was a small mom and pop place with about six tables.

The next day we were off to Ha Long Bay, which is a world heritage United Nations Educational, Scientific and Cultural Organization (UNESCO) site. Ha Long Bay has become a famous film location for several Hollywood movies. We hopped onto a boat and, as it pulled out into the bay, it was breathtaking to see the hundreds of sandstone mountains that dotted the landscape. The mountains were lined with trees and grass. It was beautiful and peaceful.

Africa

One trip we took was to the motherland, Africa, when we went to Kenya. We got off the airplane and actually kissed the ground. The workers at the airport told us, "Welcome home, brother and sister." It was a wonderful feeling.

The customs officials were not as welcoming. You see, I had a very big video camera that came disassembled into two parts (the camera itself and the VHS recording device) and was packed in a special bag fitted with foam. The customs official was concerned that I was bringing drugs into the country hidden in the equipment, and wanted to dunk the camera in water. I tried to tell him it was just a video camera, but he was suspicious because he had never seen one like it. So I hooked the camera up to the recorder, put in a VHS cassette tape, and started recording. Then I played it back for him. After that we were allowed to leave.

Patricia and I went on a safari, which included a trip to the Masai Mara, a large national game reserve near the

Serengeti. The Masai Mara is known for its lions, cheetahs, elephants and more. We stayed in a small lodge set up for the tourist trade. There were large arches formed by elephant tusks, gorilla hands turned into ashtrays, elephant foot trash cans, and stuffed tropical birds. We thought it was pretty garish.

The ground was usually so dry it was like clay powder. One night it rained very hard. The next morning Patricia and I, along with a lady with a broken leg and our driver, drove out to see wild game. We got about an hour out from camp when the Land Rover got stuck in the mud, up to its axles. The driver and I got out and tried to push, with Patricia in the driver's seat, but we were unable to get the Land Rover out the muck. The mud was so thick it was sucking my boot off of my foot. The driver spotted some bones from a wildebeest's kill and tried putting some of the carcass under the wheels for traction, but it had no effect.

It was getting hot and we had no food, just bottled water. After a few hours we started hearing hyenas and saw vultures overhead.

It was about that time that Patricia told me she had to pee.

"What do you want me to do about it?" I asked. "Go ahead."

She wanted to go somewhere that would effectively block her from view so she could maintain her modesty. Nearby was a large termite mound over six feet tall. But our driver had mentioned that lions like to lie on the shady sides of the mounds to get the cool air that flows up from underground. Patricia told me to check and see if there was a lion on the shady side of the termite mound.

I said, "And if there is a lion what am I supposed to do?"

She said, "Run." Like I can outrun a lion.

So, like the dutiful husband I am, I went to look around the mound. Thank God there was no lion, so I called

Patricia over. She did her business, then we ran back to the Land Rover.

It was eight hours before help arrived in the form of the reserve's park rangers, men who roamed the reserve hunting for poachers. Patricia had a red jacket that she had actually been told not to bring because red is the color of the Masai tribe and they might get offended by someone else wearing the color. But it was the only jacket she had, and she was always cold, so she had brought it anyway. Man, am I glad she had that coat. She got on top of the Land Rover and waved the jacket furiously while we all screamed at the tops of our lungs. The rangers spotted us, and came and pulled us out of the mud with a heavy chain.

As soon as we got back to camp, Patricia and I went straight to our lodge, thirsty, starving and exhausted. I wished we had picked a place that had showers.

John Watts in Africa

Patricia Watts in Africa

CHAPTER 45
FIGHTING FOR
MY HEALTH

As I got older the toll of the war started catching up to me on a physical level. I was diagnosed with symptoms caused by exposure to Agent Orange.

Agent Orange was a chemical herbicide and defoliant, used to clear leaves and vegetation for military operations. It got its name because the chemical was stored in barrels encircled with orange bands. During the Vietnam War the United States used it to defoliate forested land in order to deprive guerrillas of food and hiding places. It was frequently used to clear areas around military bases. It is believed that over 20% of South Vietnam's forests were sprayed at some point during the conflict.

During the war, soldiers were told that the chemical was harmless. But after the war many veterans came down with related illnesses: bladder cancer, leukemia, Hodgkin's lymphoma, Parkinson's. Children of people exposed to the chemical were born with defects.

Veterans began to file claims with the Department of Veterans Affairs in 1977, seeking medical assistance and disability payments. Claims were usually denied unless the veteran could prove that their ailments began when they were in the service, or within one year of their discharge.

For me it started as just high blood pressure. I went to a private doctor not connected to the Veterans Administration, but he linked it to my exposure to Agent Orange. The question we faced was whether the V.A. would help pay for my medical bills, as the V.A. gives compensation on a sliding scale, from 10% to 100%.

It took over three and a half years to get the V.A. to acknowledge my claim and provide medical attention which I was due. At first the V.A. told me there was no record of me being in Vietnam, and no record of me being a SEAL. The V.A. did not know for certain that I had been in-country during Vietnam. According to my records, I had only served aboard the *U.S.S. Okinawa*. But the V.A. automatically provided me medical care and treatment because I could have been exposed to Agent Orange during operations off the coast of Vietnam. They decided to cover 20% of my medical expenses.

By God's grace their testing revealed that I did not have cancer. But I did have a host of other medical problems stemming from exposure to Agent Orange. I developed diabetes, my gallbladder was taken out, I was diagnosed with a growth on my kidney that has to be monitored every year to see if it gets any bigger, and I have chronic obstructive pulmonary disease (COPD) and asthma.

That was not the only time I required medical care from the V.A. Around 2005 my nightmares about Vietnam started getting worse. My wife and my brother-in-law pushed me to go to the V.A. for help, so I started the claim process for the necessary medical treatment.

It again took years to get the V.A. to acknowledge this particular claim. Unlike the Agent Orange treatment, which was pretty much a given for anyone who was present in Vietnam, the process for PTSD treatment required my DD Form 214, Certificate of Release or Discharge from Active Duty. That document is a record that shows times and places of service, rank at discharge and job classification. But my DD214 did not have much of that information because of the secretive nature of my service as a SEAL; much of the information had been redacted from my records. So I had to prove to the V.A. that I'd been boots on the ground as a SEAL in Vietnam.

There were few friends I had left who were still alive, and I had to locate them and ask them to write letters about our time in-country. They all did this for me, but the letters were not sufficient for the V.A. and my claim was denied.

I requested my full service record and was told that there had been a fire in St. Louis, Missouri, and military records of my Team were destroyed in the fire. I started to become very disillusioned and angry with the process.

There was a deep-seated anger that only made me more short-tempered and eager to fight for myself. I continued to apply for compensation from the V.A. and I continued to be denied. I lost heart and faith in the system and started to think that I would be better off dead, and that my wife Patricia would be better off without me.

I sought the help of Senator Arlen Specter of Pennsylvania. He was kind enough to speak to me and I was able to tell him about the problem with my records.

In the interim I started to see a psychiatrist and psychologist at the V.A. hospital in Philadelphia on an outpatient basis, paying out of pocket. The psychiatrist put me through immersive therapy again, where I would focus on one incident that took place during the war. It was very rough reliving the same incident over and over and over again. It brought tears to my eyes and pain to my heart.

A month after talking to Senator Specter, he had my records in hand, along with medals I had not even known about. He had also obtained a letter from the commander of the forces in Vietnam, General William Westmoreland. The General commended me and my Team for our actions in Hue during Tet.

I was finally approved for disability. My psychologist

diagnosed me with severe PTSD and I had to be treated at the
Coatesville V.A. mental hospital for continued thoughts of
suicide.

CHAPTER 46
A LOSS NO PARENT SHOULD BEAR

Our daughter Sheralyn was beautiful. She had light brown hair and blue gray eyes. She took up with a no-good dirty dog who shall go unnamed.

One Sunday night Patricia and I were watching TV when Sherry and that asshole came in saying they had something to tell us. They had eloped and been married for two weeks. Sherry was 18, a young adult, so there was nothing I could say to her or him. But it broke our hearts knowing she had married this nothing of a man.

Sherry had already had a son, Shawn Nelson Fortune, who was four years old when she married the piece of shit. Patricia and I helped the three of them get their first apartment and got them settled in. They were evicted from the apartment within six months, and they moved in with his mother. Over the next eight years of their marriage, we were often called by our daughter asking for help. She was physically afraid of him, but she just would never leave him. After four years they had a daughter, her name was Saliemah.

As time went on their marriage did not get any better. On January 6, 1990, when Sherry was 26, she and Shawn and Saliemah had dinner with us. Sherry decided that she'd had enough and was going to leave her husband, who was trying to become a Muslim at the time.

Sherry asked to borrow one of our cars to take the kids back to their apartment and pick up a few things. Patricia and I waited for them to come back by watching a James Bond movie on TV. About an hour into the movie, we got a phone call from Shawn. He was crying and said his mom was locked in the bedroom. He banged on the door, but Sherry did not answer him.

We got in our other car and I drove like a bat out of hell to our daughter's apartment. When we got there the kids were on the sofa in their pajamas. Patricia went up the stairs to the bedroom. We called out to our daughter but there was no answer. There was a new padlock on the door, so I slammed it with my shoulder and the door gave in. We walked in to see the room was a wreck. The mattress was upside down. I lifted the mattress and there she was, our daughter, with a 10-inch butcher's knife in her back. Patricia turned her over and performed CPR, even though the entire time she knew our daughter was with Jesus.

Her scumbag husband had taken all her jewelry and ran out of the house, leaving the kids in a cold living room with their dead mother's body upstairs.

We called the police, and Patricia, the kids and I were each interviewed separately, each for over an hour. The next day the city coroner pronounced our daughter's death a murder.

The next day was a Sunday. I don't know what possessed me to go into work, my part-time job at a video rental store called West Coast Video. I told my good friend and coworker, Michael Katz, what had happened. I expressed how frustrated I was being unable to do anything. I wanted to find the bastard and take the law into my own hands. Mike talked me off the ledge, as it were. He told me to let law enforcement do their job. He had faith that the police would find him and bring him to justice.

The murderer had pawned the jewelry he had taken from Sherry and bought a ticket for a Greyhound bus to

Pittsburgh. Every day he would call Patricia at her job to torture her by playing "Taps" on the telephone buttons. Patricia's supervisor was a witness who testified to this in court.

This went on for a full week, with the bastard threatening to attend the funeral. But just before the funeral he gave himself up to the police. The legal process was slow, but he was found guilty of second-degree murder and sentenced to life without parole plus 30 years.

Shawn and Saliemah came to live with us immediately and we treated them as if they were our own children. Mike Katz graduated law school and passed the bar, and one of the first things he did was go to court for us to sever the father's parental rights. After that process was complete, Mike also got the court to officially change Shawn and Saliemah's last name to Watts.

Sheralyn Watts

Saliemah Watts | Shawn Watts,US Marine Corps

Zakia Watts,US Navy

CHAPTER 47
KEYS TO SUCCESS

In my mind's eye, I can still visualize myself as that curious little boy who wanted to explore the world with his shenanigans. Who knew back then that my journey would transform me completely, and I would grow up to be the extraordinarily strong and tough man that I am today?

I think the best thing that I ever did for myself was to practice self-belief every day and have faith in my journey. I had a strong intuition that my hard work was surely going to pay off someday, and I was going to achieve whatever I had always wanted to.

People say that it comes down to fate, family background, resources, or connections that make some of us more successful than others, but I don't agree with that. I believe that these factors do contribute to a person's success, but only about 20 percent; the remaining 80 percent to becoming successful or achieving something significant is to have faith in yourself. Once you start believing in yourself, no barrier is insurmountable. Your willpower and strength are the key ingredients because you can never achieve your goals if you keep doubting yourself.

Throughout my life, I have been bullied a million times for being Black; I remember those mean eyes and facial expressions that clearly stated that I was not their equal. But I always kept my head high and remained confident in my skin, regardless of the criticism. I never let that discrimination get on my nerves because I knew that I had been sent to this world to carry out a purpose that nobody else had.

If you truly want to put yourself on the track to success, you need to understand that your brain will always play against you before doing something big. I remember all those times in my teen years when I used to doubt my abilities and think that maybe I was not as capable as other people to achieve my goals. However, with time, I thankfully began to realize my worth and successfully got rid of all the procrastination, self-doubt, negative thinking and anxiety from my life. And ever since, there has been no looking back.

The next generation

CHAPTER 48

HISTORY LESSON

Where there were originally two Teams of Navy SEALs, there are now more than ten. They are still primarily organized between West Coast and East Coast.

Based at the Naval Amphibious Base Coronado in California are SEAL Teams ONE, THREE, FIVE, AND SEVEN. SEAL Team ONE's mission focus is still Southeast Asia. SEAL Team THREE focuses its missions in Southwest Asia. SEAL Team FIVE's area of focus is the Northern Pacific. SEAL Team SEVEN can conduct worldwide activities.

Then there is SEAL Team 17, also based in Coronado, California. It consists of two platoons of reservists and can be deployed anywhere in the world.

SEAL Teams TWO, FOUR, EIGHT, and TEN are based at Naval Amphibious Base Little Creek in Virginia. SEAL Team TWO concentrates on European missions. SEAL Team FOUR concentrates its activities in Central and South America. SEAL Team EIGHT focuses on the Caribbean, Africa, and the Mediterranean. SEAL Team TEN deals with the Middle East.

There is also SEAL Team 18, based in Virginia Beach, Virginia. It consists of two platoons of reservists and can be deployed anywhere in the world.

Finally, there is SEAL Team SIX, considered a thing unto

its own. It was formally commissioned in November of 1980 but in 1987 it was technically dissolved. Its successor is the Naval Special Warfare Development Group, also known as just Development Group or DEVGRU for short (although it is still often referred to by its SEAL Team SIX appellation or sometimes Task Force Blue). DEVGRU is still composed solely of Navy SEALs. The group is based out of Virginia Beach, Virginia.

DEVGRU is supported by Naval Special Warfare Command and assigned to Joint Special Operations Command. Most information concerning DEVGRU is classified, but it functions as the Navy's primary special missions unit, performing counter-terrorism, hostage rescue, special reconnaissance, and offensive actions against high value targets.

There are two Teams of what could be considered underwater specialists: SEAL Delivery Vehicle Team ONE (stationed in Pearl Harbor, Hawaii and operating in the Indian and Pacific Oceans and the Middle East) and SEAL Delivery Vehicle Team TWO (headquartered at Virginia Beach, Virginia and operating in the Atlantic Ocean, Europe, and North and South America). SEAL Delivery Vehicles consist of manned submersibles and swimmer delivery vehicles. They are primarily used for covert missions, including placing mines on ships.

The Brotherhood

It is still difficult to get accepted into the Navy's SEAL training program, even more difficult to pass the grueling process and become one. But it is just as much a symbol of pride to be a Navy SEAL. I will be forever proud, and forever grateful, for the opportunity to serve and for the brothers I made.

ABOUT THE AUTHORS

John Watts was one of the first Black Navy SEALs. *Shadow S.E.A.L.* spans from his youth, through his military training, to his years serving in Vietnam, as well as his attempts to get his life back on track after coming home. This is his first book.

Michael S. Katz has been a professional author, ghost writer, and editor since 2002. He has worked with best-selling authors and on award-winning books. His works include fiction and non-fiction.

CPSIA information can be obtained
at www.ICGtesting.com
Printed in the USA
LVHW081339191122
733280LV00025B/1671

9 781932 045338